MAMMOTH

Book I: SILVERHAIR

Also by Stephen Baxter

THE XEELEE SEQUENCE

Raft
Timelike Infinity
Flux
Ring
Vacuum Diagrams (short stories)

OTHER TITLES

Anti-Ice
The Time Ships
Titan
Voyage
Moonseed
Traces (short stories)

FOR YOUNGER READERS

Gulliverzone
Webcrash

MAMMOTH

Book 1: SILVERHAIR

Stephen Baxter

MILLENNIUM

First published in Great Britain in 1999 by
Millennium
An imprint of the Orion Publishing Company Ltd
Orion House, 5 Upper St Martin's Lane
London WC2H 9EA

A CIP catalogue record for this book is
available from the British Library

Typeset in Great Britain at
The Spartan Press Ltd,
Lymington, Hants,
Printed and bound by
Clays Ltd, St Ives plc.

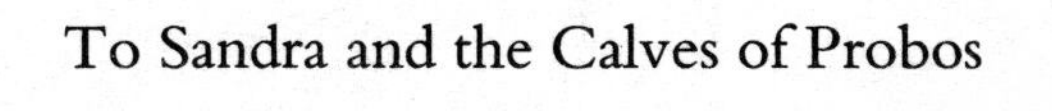

To Sandra and the Calves of Probos

PROLOGUE

It is a frozen world.

To the south there are forests. But to the north, the trees – hundred-year-old spruce barely six feet tall, stunted by cold and wind – grow ever more thinly scattered, until they peter out altogether.

And beyond, where it is too cold for the hardiest tree, there is only the tundra: an immense, undulating plain, a white monotony broken by splinters of rock. Very little snow falls here, but unimpeded winds whip up ice crystals, giving the illusion of frequent blizzards. Even the outcropping rock has been shattered by millennia of frost to a rough, unstable scree.

Under the silent stars nothing stirs but the ruffled surface of the larger lakes, tormented by the breeze. The smaller lakes are frozen completely. From this place there is nothing but snow and ice and frozen ocean, all the way to the North Pole.

It seems impossible that anything should live here. And yet there is life.

There are birds here: snowy owls and ptarmigan, able to survive the bleakest midwinter by sheltering in holes in the snow. And later in the season many thousands more birds will migrate here from their winter homes across the planet. More life, plant and animal, lies dormant under the snow, waiting for the brief glory of summer. And to the north, on the frozen ocean itself, live polar bears and their prey: sea mammals like seals and walrus.

. . . And there is more.

The stars are scintillating now. A vicious wind is rising, and the ice fields to the north are shrouded in a grey haze.

And out of that haze something looms: a mountainous shape, seemingly too massive to move, and yet move it does. As it approaches through the obscuring mist, more of its form becomes visible: a body round as an eroded rock, head dropped down before it as it probes for saxifrage buds beneath the snow, the whole covered in a layer of thick red-brown hair.

The great head rears up. A trunk comes questing, and immense tusks sweep. An eye opens, warm, brown, intense, startlingly human.

This is not a vision from prehistory. This is real: a living thing a hundred times as massive as any human, a living thing prospering in this frozen desert.

The great trunk lifts, and the woolly mammoth trumpets her ancient songs of blood and wisdom.

Her name is Silverhair.

ONE

FAMILY

THE STORY OF THE HOTBLOODS

The first Cycle story of all (Silverhair told Icebones, her calf) – the *very* first of all – is of long, long ago, when there were no mammoths.

In fact there were no wolves or birds or seals or bears.

For the world belonged to the Reptiles.

Now, the Reptiles were the greatest beasts ever seen – so huge they made the Earth itself shake with their footfalls – and they were cunning and savage hunters.

But they didn't have things all their own way.

Our ancestors called themselves the Hotbloods.

The Hotbloods were small, timid creatures who lived underground, in burrows, the way lemmings do. The ancestors of every warm-blood creature you see today lived in those cramped dens: bear with seal, wolf with mammoth. They had huge, frightened eyes, for they would only emerge from their burrows at night, a time when the Reptiles were less active and less able to hunt them. They all looked alike, and rarely even argued, for their world was dominated by the constant threat of the Reptiles.

That was the way the world had been for ten thousand Great-Years.

It was into this world that Kilukpuk, the first of all Matriarchs, was born. If you could have seen her, small and cautious like the rest, you would never have imagined the mighty races which would one day spring from her loins. But, despite her smallness, Kilukpuk was destined to become the mother of us all.

Now Kilukpuk had a brother, called Aglu. He was hard-eyed and selfish, and was often accused of hiding when foraging parties were being readied, and of stealing others' food – even stealing from infants. But Aglu was sly, and nothing was ever proven.

Despite his faults, Kilukpuk loved her brother. She defended him from attack, and did not complain when he took the warmest place in the burrow, or stole her food, for she always dreamed he would learn the error of his ways.

Now, there came a time when a great light appeared in the night sky.

It was a ball of grey-white, and it had a huge hairy tail that streamed away from the sun. The light was beautiful, but it was deadly, for it turned night to day, and made it easy for the Reptiles to pick off the foraging Hotbloods. Great was the mourning in the burrows.

One night Kilukpuk was out alone, digging in a mound of Reptile dung for undigested nuts – when suddenly . . .

Well, Kilukpuk never knew what happened, and I don't suppose any of us will.

The Earth trembled. There was a great glow, as if dawn was approaching – but the glow was in the *west*, not the east. Clouds boiled across the sky.

Then the sky itself started to burn, and a great hail of shooting stars poured down towards the land, coming from the west.

Kilukpuk felt a new shaking of the ground. Silhouetted against the red fire glow of the west, she saw Reptiles: thousands, millions of them – and they were running.

The Reptiles had ruled the world as gods. But now they were fleeing in panic.

Kilukpuk ran back to her burrow, convinced that if even the gods were so afraid, she and her Family were sure to die.

The days that followed were filled with strangeness and terror.

A great heat swept over the land.

Then a rain began, salty and heavy, so powerful it was as if an ocean was emptying itself over their heads.

And then the clouds came, and snow fell even at the height of summer.

Kilukpuk and her Family, starved and thirsty, thought this was the end of all things. But their burrows protected the Hotbloods, while the creatures of the surface perished.

At last the cold abated, and day and night returned to the world.

No Reptiles came. There were no footfalls, no digging claws, no bellows of frustrated hunters.

At last, one night, Kilukpuk and Aglu led a party to the surface.

They found a world that was all but destroyed. The trees and bushes had been smashed down by winds and burned by fire.

There were no Reptiles, anywhere.

But the Hotbloods found food to eat in the ruined world, for they were used to living off scraps anyhow. There were roots, and bark that wasn't too badly burned, and the first green shoots of recovering plants.

Soon the Hotbloods grew fat, and, without the ground-rattling footfalls of the Reptiles to disturb them, began to sleep well during the long, hot days of that strange time.

But there came a time when some Hotbloods did not return from the nightly foraging expeditions, just as it had been before. And then, one day, Kilukpuk was wakened from a dreamless sleep by a *slam-slam-slam* that shook dirt from the roofs of the burrows.

Aglu, her brother, came running through the burrows. 'It is the Reptiles! They have returned!'

Kilukpuk gathered her calves to her. They were terrified and bewildered.

After that, things rapidly got worse. More foragers were lost on the surface. The Hotbloods became as fearful and hollow-eyed as they had ever been, and food soon began to run short in the burrows.

But Kilukpuk could not help but notice that not all the Hotbloods were suffering so. While the others were skinny and raddled by disease, Aglu and his band of companions seemed sleek and healthy. Kilukpuk grew suspicious, though her suspicion saddened her, for she still loved her brother deeply.

At last, one night, she followed Aglu and his companions to the surface. She saw that Aglu and the others made little effort to conceal themselves – in fact they laughed and cavorted in the Moonlight.

And then they did a very strange thing.

When they had eaten their fill of the roots and green plants, Aglu and his friends climbed up low bushes and hurled themselves at the ground. They pushed pebbles off low outcrops and let them dash against the ground. They even picked up heavy branches and slammed them against the ground – all the time roaring and howling as if they were Reptiles themselves.

And, when an unwary Hotblood came poking her nose out of the ground, Aglu and his friends prepared to attack her.

Immediately Kilukpuk rose up with a roar of rage. She fell on Aglu and his followers, cuffing and kicking and biting them, scattering their pebbles and their sticks.

The Hotblood whose life had been spared ran away. Aglu's followers soon fled, leaving Kilukpuk facing her brother. She picked him up by the scruff of his neck. 'So,' she said, 'you are the mighty Reptile that has terrified my calves.'

'Let me go, Kilukpuk,' he said, wriggling. 'The Reptiles have gone. We are free—'

'Free to enslave your Cousins with fear? I should rip you to pieces myself.'

Aglu grew frightened. 'Spare me, Kilukpuk. I am your brother.'

And Kilukpuk said, 'I will spare you. For Hotblood should not kill Hotblood. But you are no brother of mine; and your mouth and fur stink of blood. Go now.'

And she threw him as hard as she could, threw him so far his body flew over the horizon, his cries diminishing.

She went back to the burrows to comfort her calves, and tell her people the danger was over: that they need not skulk in their burrows, that they could live on the land, not under it, and they could enjoy the light of day, not cower in darkness.

And Kilukpuk led her people to the sunlit land, and they began to feed on the new plants that sprouted from the richness of the burned ground.

As for Aglu, some say he was ripped apart and eaten by his own calves, and they have never forgotten the taste of that grisly repast: for they became the bear and the wolf, and the other Hotbloods which eat their own kind.

Certainly Kilukpuk never gave up her vigilance, even as she grew strong and sleek, and her fertile loins poured forth generation after generation of calves. And her calves feared nobody.

Nobody, that is, except the Lost.

Chapter One

THE HEADLAND

Silverhair, standing tall on the headland, was cupped in a land of flatness: a land of far horizons, a land of blue and grey, of fog and rain, of watery light no brighter than an English winter twilight.

It was the will of Kilukpuk, of course, that Silverhair should be the first to spot the Lost. Nobody but Silverhair – Silverhair the rebel, the Cow who behaved more like a musth Bull, as Owlheart would tell her – nobody but her would even have been standing here, alone, on this headland at the south-western corner of the Island, looking out to sea with her trunk raised to test the air.

The dense Arctic silence was abruptly broken by the evocative calls of birds. Silverhair saw them on the cliff below her, prospecting for their colony: the first kittiwakes, arriving from the south. It was a sign of life, a sign of spring, and she felt her own spirits rise in response.

A few paces from Silverhair, in a hollow near the cliff edge, a solid bank of snow had gathered. Now a broad, claw-tipped paw broke its way out into the open air, and beady black eyes and nose protruded. It was a polar bear: a female. The bear climbed out, a mountain of yellow-white fur. Lean after consuming her body fat over the winter, her strong, elegant neck jutted forward; her muscles, long and flowing, worked as she glided over the crusted snow.

The bear saw Silverhair. She fixed the huge mammoth with a glare, quite fearless.

Then she stretched, circled and clambered back in through the narrow hole to the cubs she had borne during the winter, leaving a hind leg waving in the air.

Amused, Silverhair looked to the south.

The black bulk of a spruce forest obscured her view of the coast itself – and of the mysterious Nest of Straight Lines which stood there, a place which could be glimpsed only when the air was clear of fog or mist or snow, a sinister place which no mammoth would willingly visit. But Silverhair could see beyond the forest, to the ocean itself.

Here and there blown snow snaked across the landfast ice that fringed the Island's coast. Two pairs of black guillemots, striking in their winter plumage, swam along the sea edge, mirrored in the calm water. Pack ice littered the Channel that lay between Island and Mainland. The ice had been smashed and broken by the wind; the glistening blue-white sheet was pocked by holes and leads exposing black, surging water.

Away from the shore the sea, of course, remained open, as it did all year round, swept clear of ice by the powerful currents that surged there. Frost-smoke rose from the open water, turned to gold by the low sun. And beyond the Channel, twilight was gathering on that mysterious Mainland itself. It was the land from which – according to mammoth legend recorded in the Cycle – the great hero

Longtusk had, long ago, evacuated his Family to save them from extinction.

And as the day waned, she could see the strange gathering of lights, there on the Mainland: like stars, a crowded constellation, but these lights were orange and yellow and unwinking, and they clung to the ground like lichen. Silverhair growled and squinted, but her vision was poor. If only she could *smell* that remote place; if only it sent out deep contact rumbles rather than useless slivers of light.

And now heavy storm clouds descended on that unattainable land, obscuring the light.

In the icy breeze, the air crackled in her nostrils, and her breath froze in the fur that covered her face.

That was when she saw the Lost.

She didn't know what she was seeing then, of course.

All she saw was something adrift on the sea between the Island and Mainland. At first she thought it was just an ice floe; perhaps those unmoving shapes on the top of the floe were seals, resting as they chewed on their monotonous diet of fish and birds.

But she had never seen seals sitting up as these creatures did, never seen seals with fins as long and splayed as these – never heard voices, floating over the water and the shore of ice and rock, as petulant and peevish as these.

Even the 'ice floe' was strange, its sides and one end straight, the other end coming to a point like a tusk's, its middle hollow, cupping the seal-like creatures inside. Whatever it was, it was drifting steadily closer to the Island; it would surely come to ground somewhere south of the spruce forest, and spill those squabbling creatures on the shore there.

She knew she should return to the Family, tell them what she had seen. Perhaps Owlheart or Eggtusk, in their age and wisdom – or clever Lop-ear, she thought warmly – would know the meaning of this. But she had time to watch a little longer, to indulge the curiosity that had already caused her so much trouble during her short life.

. . . But now she heard the stomping.

It was a deep pounding, surging through the rocky ground. A human would have heard nothing, not even felt the quiver of the ground caused by those great footfalls. But Silverhair recognised it immediately, for the stomping has the longest range of all the mammoths' means of calling each other.

This was the distinctive footfall of Owlheart herself: it was the Matriarch, calling her Family together. The birth must be near.

When Silverhair had been a calf, the Island had rung to the stomping of mammoths, for there were many Families in those days, scattered across the tundra. Now there was only the remote echo of her own Matriarch's footfall. But Silverhair – nervous about the birth to come, curiosity engaged by what she had seen today – did not reflect long on this.

The new spring sun was weak, a red ball that rolled along the horizon, offering little warmth. And already, heartbreakingly soon, it was setting, having shed little heat over the snow which still covered the ground. The last light turned the mountains pink, and it caught Silverhair's loose outer fur, making it glow, so that it was as if she was surrounded by a smoky halo.

She stole one last glimpse at the strange object in the sea. It had almost passed out of sight anyway, as it drifted away from the headland.

She turned and began her journey back to her Family.

Later she would wonder if it might have been better to have

ignored the Matriarch's call, descended to the shore – and, without mercy, destroyed the strange object and the creatures it contained.

Chapter Two

THE BIRTH

Mammoths wander. Few wander as far as Silverhair did, however.

It took her ten days to cross the Island and return to the northern tundra where her Family was gathered. She was not aware of the way the ground itself shuddered as her feet passed, and the way lemmings were rattled in their winter burrows in the snow. But the rodents were unconcerned, and went about their tiny businesses without interruption. For they knew that the mammoths, the greatest creatures in the land, would do them no harm.

Silverhair knew that the worst of the winter was over: that time of perpetual night broken only by the occasional flare of the aurora borealis, the time of the hard winds from the north that drove snow and ice crystals before them. The return of the sun had been heralded by days in which the darkness was relieved by twilight, when the black star pool above had turned to a dome of glowing purple – purple enriched by swathes of blue, pink, even some flashes of green – before sinking back to darkness again, all without a sliver of sunlight.

But every day the noon twilights had grown longer and stronger, until at last the sun itself had come peeking over the horizon. At first it was just a splinter of blinding light that quickly disappeared, as if shy. But at last it had climbed fully above the horizon, for the first time for more than a hundred days.

In the new light, to the north, she could see the sweep of the Island itself. The tundra was still largely buried in pale snow and ice, with none of the rich marsh green or splashes of flowering colour that the growth of summer would bring. And beyond, to the farthest north, she could see the bony faces of the Mountains at the End of the World, looming out of the bluish mist that lingered there, brown cones striped by the great white glaciers that spilled from rocky valleys. The Mountains were a wall of ice and rock beyond which no mammoth had ever ventured.

Along the south coast of the Island, more sheltered, the oily green-black of a spruce forest clung to the rock. The trees were intruders, encroaching on the ancient tundra which provided Silverhair's Family with the grassy food they needed.

Despite her sense of urgency, Silverhair paused frequently to feed. Her trunk was busy and active, like an independent creature, as it worked at the ground. She would wrap her trunk-fingers around the sparse tufts of grass she found under the snow, cramming the dark-green goodies into her small mouth, and grind them between her great molar teeth with a back-and-forth movement of her jaw. The grass, the last of the winter, was coarse, dry and unsatisfying, as was the rest of her diet of twigs and bark of birches, willows and larches; with a corner of her mind she looked forward to her richer summer feast to come.

And she would lift her anus flap and pass dung, briskly and efficiently, as mammoths must ten or twelve times a day. The soft brown mass settled to the ice behind her, steaming; it would enrich the soil it touched, and the seeds that had passed through Silverhair's stomach would germinate and turn the land green.

The Family had no permanent home. They would gather to migrate to new pastures, or when one of their members was in some difficulty. But they would scatter in pairs or small groups to forage for food during the day, or to sleep at night. There was never any formal arrangement about where to meet again – nor was one necessary, for the mammoths were by far the most massive beasts in the landscape, and the authoritative stomping of Owlheart, and the rumbling and calls of the Family gathered together, travelled – to a mammoth's ears – from one end of the Island to another.

On the eighth day, a line of white vapour cut across the deep blue sky, utterly straight, feathering slightly. Silverhair peered upward; the vapour trail was at the limit of her poor vision. There was a tiny, glittering form at the head of the vapour line, like a high-flying bird, but its path was unnaturally straight and unwavering, its wings stiff, as if frozen. And a sound like remote thunder came drifting down, even though there wasn't a cloud in the sky.

Silverhair had seen such things before. Nobody could tell her what it was, what it meant. After a time, the glittering mote passed out of sight, and the vapour trail slowly dispersed.

On the ninth day Silverhair was able to hear, not just the Matriarch's stomping, but also the rumbles, trumpets and growls of her people. The deep voices of mammoths – too deep for human ears – will carry far across the land, unimpeded by grassland, snow banks, even forest.

And in the evening of that day, when the wind was right, she could smell home: the rich, hot smell of fresh dung, the musk stink of wet fur.

On the tenth day she was able to see the others at last. The mammoths, gathered together, were blocky shapes looming out of the blue-tinged fog. Silverhair was something of a loner, but even so she felt her heart pump, her blood flow warm in her veins, at the thought of greeting the Family.

Warm at the thought – she admitted it – of seeing Lop-ear once more.

The mammoths were scraping away thin layers of snow with their feet and tusks to get at the saxifrage buds below. Moulting winter fur hung around them in untidy clouds, and she could see how gaunt they were, after a winter spent burning the fat of the long-gone summer. It had been a hard winter, even for this frozen desert, and standing water had been unusually difficult to find. Silverhair knew that when the weather lifted – and if the thaw did not come soon – the Matriarch would have to lead them to seek open water. It would be an arduous trek, and there was no guarantee of success, but there might be no choice.

The Family's two adult Bulls came to meet her.

Here was powerful old Eggtusk, his ears ragged from the many battles he had fought, and with the strange egg-shaped ivory growth in his tusk that had given him his name. And here, too, was Lop-ear, the younger Bull, with his dangling, parasite-damaged ear. The Bulls were launching into their greeting ceremony, and Silverhair joined in, rumbling and trumpeting, excited despite the shortness of her separation.

The three mammoths raised their trunks and tails and ran and spun around. They urinated and defecated in a tight ring, their dung merging in a circle of brown warmth on the ground. Old Eggtusk was the clumsiest of the three, of course, but what he lacked in elegance he made up for in his massive enthusiasm.

And now they touched each other. Silverhair clicked tusks with Eggtusk, and – with more enthusiasm – touched Lop-ear's face and mouth, wrapping her trunk over his head and rubbing at his scalp hair. She found the musth glands in his cheeks and slowly snaked her trunk across them, reading his subtle chemical language, while he rubbed her forehead; and then they pulled back their trunks and entangled them in a tight knot.

A human observer would have seen only three mammoths dancing in their baffling circles, trumpeting and growling and stomping, even emitting high-pitched, bird-like squeaks with their trunks. Perhaps, with patience, she might have deduced some simple patterns: the humming sound that indicated a warning, a roar that was a signal to attack, the whistling that meant that one of the Family was injured or in distress.

But mammoth speech is based not just on the sounds mammoths make – from the ground-shaking stomps, through low-pitched rumbles, bellows, trumpets and growls, to the highest chirrups of their trunks – but also on the complex dances of their bodies, and changes in how they smell or breathe or scratch, even in the deep throb of their pulses. All of this makes mammoth speech richer than any human language.

'. . . Hello!' Silverhair was calling. 'Hello! I'm so glad to see you! Hello!'

'Silverhair,' Eggtusk growled, failing to mask his pleasure at seeing her again. 'Last back as usual. By Kilukpuk's mite-ridden left ear, I swear you're more Bull than Cow.'

'Oh, Eggtusk, you can't keep that up.' And she laid her trunk over Eggtusk's head and began to tickle him behind his ear with her delicate trunk-fingers. 'Plenty of mites in this ear too.'

He growled in pleasure and shook his head; his hair, matted with mud, moved in great lanks over his eyes. 'You won't be able to run away when you have your own calf. You just bear that in mind. You should be watching and learning from your sister.'

'I know, I know,' she said. But she kept up her tickling, for she knew his scolding wasn't serious. A new birth was too rare and infrequent an event for anyone to maintain ill humour for long.

Rare and infrequent – but not so rare as what she'd seen on the sea, she thought, remembering. 'Lop-ear. You've got to come with me.' She wrapped her trunk around his and tugged.

He laughed, and flicked back his lifeless ear. 'What is it, Silverhair?'

'I saw the strangest thing in the sea. To the south, from the headland. It was like an ice floe – but it wasn't; it was too dark for that. And there were animals on it – or rather inside it – like seals—'

Lop-ear was watching her fondly. He was a year older than Silverhair. Although he wouldn't reach his full height until he was forty years old, he was already tall, and his shoulders were broad and strong, and his brown eyes like pools of autumn sunlight.

But Eggtusk snorted. 'By Kilukpuk's snot-crusted nostril, what are you talking about, Silverhair? Why can't you wander off and find something useful – like nice warm water for us to drink?'

'The animals were cupped inside the floating thing, for it was hollow, like—' She had no language to describe what she'd seen. So she released Lop-ear's trunk and ripped a fingerful of trampled grass from the ground. Carefully, sheltering the blades from the wind, she cupped the grass. 'Like this!'

Lop-ear looked puzzled.

Eggtusk was frowning. '*Seals*, you say?'

'But they weren't seals,' she said. 'They had four flippers each – or rather, legs – that were stuck out at angles, like broken twigs. And heads, big round heads . . . You do believe me, don't you?'

Eggtusk was serious now. He said, 'I don't like the sound of that. Not one bit.'

Silverhair didn't understand. 'Why not?'

But now, from the circle of Cows, Foxeye, her sister, cried out.

Lop-ear pushed Silverhair's backside, gently, with his trunk. 'Go on, Silverhair. You can't stay with us Bulls. Your place is with your sister.'

And so Silverhair, with a mix of fascination and reluctance, walked to the centre of the Family, where the Cows were gathered around her sister.

At the heart of the group was massive Owlheart – Silverhair's grandmother, the Matriarch of them all – and like a shadow behind her was Wolfnose. Wolfnose, Owlheart's mother, had once been Matriarch, but now she was so old that her name, given her for the sharpness of her sense of smell as a calf, seemed no more than a sad joke.

And before Owlheart's tree-trunk legs was a Cow, lying on her side on the ground. It was Foxeye, Silverhair's sister, who was close to birthing.

Owlheart lifted her great head and fixed Silverhair with a steady, intense glare; for a few heartbeats Silverhair saw in her the ghost of the patient predator bird after whom the Matriarch had been named. 'Silverhair! Where have you been?' She added such a deep rumble to her voice that Silverhair felt her chest quiver.

'To the headland. I was just—'

'I don't care,' said Owlheart. Given the question, it wasn't a logical answer. But then, Silverhair reflected, if you're the Matriarch, you don't have to be logical.

Now Snagtooth – Silverhair's aunt, Owlheart's daughter – was standing before her. 'About time, Silverhair,' she snapped, and she spat out a bit of enamel that had broken off the misshapen molar that was growing out of the left side of her mouth. Snagtooth was tall for a Cow: big, intimidating, unpredictably angry.

'Leave me alone, Snagtooth.'

Croptail came pushing his way between Snagtooth's legs to Silverhair. 'Silverhair! Silverhair!' Croptail was Foxeye's first calf. He was a third-molar – on his third set of teeth – born ten years earlier, a skinny, uncertain ball of orange hair with a peculiar stub of a tail. Kept away from his mother during the birth, he looked lost and frightened. 'I'm hungry, Silverhair.' He pushed his mouth into her fur, looking for her nipples.

Gently she tried to nudge him away. 'I can't feed you, child.'

The little Bull's voice was plaintive. 'But Momma is sick.'

'No she isn't. But when she has the new baby, you'll have to feed yourself. You'll have to find grass and—'

But Snagtooth was still growling at Silverhair. 'You always were unreliable. My sister would be ashamed.'

Silverhair squared up to her sour-eyed aunt. 'Don't you talk about my mother.'

'I'll say what I like.'

'It's only because you can't have calves of your own, no matter how many Bulls you take. That's why you're as bitter as last summer's bark. Everybody knows it.'

'Why, you little—'

Owlheart stepped between them, her great trunk working back and forth. 'Are you two Bulls in musth? Snagtooth, take the calf.'

'But she—'

Owlheart reared up to her full height, and towered over Snagtooth. 'Do not question me, daughter. Take him.'

Snagtooth subsided. She dug an impatient trunk into the mat

of fur under Silverhair's belly, and pulled out a squealing Croptail.

At last, Silverhair was able to reach Foxeye. Her sister was lying on her side, her back legs flexing uncomfortably, the swell in her belly obvious. Her fur was muddy and matted with dew and sweat.

Silverhair entwined her trunk with her sister's. 'I'm sorry I'm so late.'

'Don't be,' said Foxeye weakly. Her small, sharp eyes were, today, brown pools of tears, and the dugs that protruded from the damp, flattened fur over her chest were swollen with milk. 'I wish Mother was here.'

Silverhair's grip tightened. 'So do I.'

The pregnancy had taken almost two full years. Foxeye's mate had been a Bull from Lop-ear's bachelor herd – and that, Silverhair thought uneasily, was the last time any of them had seen a mammoth from outside the Family. Foxeye had striven to time her pregnancy so that her calf would be born in the early spring, with a full season of plant growth and feeding ahead of it before the winter closed around them once more. It had been a long, difficult gestation, with Foxeye often falling ill; but at last, it seemed, her day had come.

The great, stolid legs of Owlheart and Wolfnose stood over Foxeye, and Silverhair felt a huge reassurance that the older Cows were here to help her sister, as they had helped so many mothers before – including her own.

Foxeye's legs kicked back, and she cried out.

Silverhair stepped back, alarmed. 'Is it time?'

Owlheart laid a strong, soothing trunk on Foxeye's back. 'Don't be afraid, Silverhair. Watch now.'

The muscles of Foxeye's stomach flexed in great waves. And then, with startling suddenness, it began.

A pink-purple foetal sac thrust out of Foxeye's body. The sac was small, streamlined like a seal, and glistening with fluid. As it pushed in great surges from Foxeye's pink warmth it looked more like something from the sea, thought Silverhair, than mammoth blood and bone.

One last heave, and Foxeye expelled the sac. It dropped with a liquid noise to the ground.

Owlheart stepped forward. With clean, confident swipes of her tusks she began to cut open the foetal sac and strip it away.

Foxeye shuddered once more. The afterbirth was expelled, a steaming, bloody mass of flesh. Then Foxeye fell back against the hard, cold ground, closing her eyes, her empty belly heaving with her deep, exhausted breaths.

Silverhair watched, fascinated, as the new calf emerged from its sac. The trunk came first, a thin, dark rope. Then came the head, for a moment protruding almost comically from the sac. It was plastered with pale-orange hair, soaked with blood and amniotic fluid, and it turned this way and that. Two eyes opened, and they were bright-pink discs; then the tiny mouth popped moistly open under the waving trunk.

'Her eyes,' Silverhair said softly.

Wolfnose, her great-grandmother, was stroking and soothing Foxeye. 'What about her eyes?'

'They're *red*.'

'So they should be. Everything is as it should be, as it has been since Kilukpuk birthed her last calves in the Swamp.'

The baby was a small bundle of bloody, matted fur, sprawled on the grass. She breathed with wet sucking noises, and her breath steamed; she let out a thin wail of protest and began to scrabble at the ground with her stumpy legs.

Owlheart's trunk tapped Silverhair's flank. 'Help her, child.'

Silverhair stepped forward nervously. She lowered her trunk and wrapped it around the calf's belly. Her skin was hot, and slick with birthing fluid that was already gathering frost. With gentle pulling, Silverhair helped the infant to stagger to her feet. The calf looked about blindly, mewling.

An infant mammoth, at birth, is already three feet tall. A human baby's body weighs less than the mammoth's brain.

'She wants her first suck,' Owlheart said softly.

With gentle tugs Silverhair guided the stumbling infant forward.

Foxeye knelt and stood, uncertainly, so that her pendulous dugs hung down before the calf. Silverhair slid her trunk under the calf's chin, and helped the calf roll her tiny trunk on to her forehead. Soon the baby's pink mouth had found her mother's nipple.

'Red eyes,' said Foxeye. 'Like the rising sun. That's her name. *Sunfire.*'

Then Silverhair, with Owlheart and Wolfnose, stood by the calf and mother. They kept the infant warm with their bodies, and used their trunks to clean the baby as she stood amid the rich hair of her mother's belly, protected by the palisade of their huge legs around her. After a time Foxeye moved away from the reaching calf, encouraging her to walk after her.

And, as she watched the infant suckle, Silverhair felt an odd pressure in her own empty dugs.

At the end of the long night, with the deep purple of dawn seeping into the eastern sky, Silverhair broke away from the Cows so she could feed and pass dung.

Wolfnose came wandering over the uneven tundra.

Silverhair, moved by an obscure concern, followed her great-grandmother.

The old Cow, her hair clumpy and matted, tugged fitfully at the trampled grass. But the co-ordination of her trunk-fingers was poor, and the wiry grass blades evaded her. Even when she managed to drag a fingerful from the hard, frozen ground and crammed it in her mouth, Silverhair could see that much of the crushed grass was spilling from her mouth, and a greenish juice trickled over her lower lip.

Silverhair, tenderly, reached forward and tucked the grass back into Wolfnose's mouth.

Wolfnose was so old now that the two great molars in her jaw – her last set – were wearing down, and soon they would no longer be able to perform the job of grinding her food. Then, no matter what the Family did for her, Wolfnose's ribs and backbone would become even more visible through her sagging flesh and clumps of hair. And, if the wolves spared her, her rheumy eyes would close for the last time.

It would be a time of sadness. But it was as it had been since the days of Kilukpuk.

Wolfnose was mumbling, even as her great jaw scraped ineffectually at the grass. 'Too long,' she said. 'Too long.'

'Too long since what?' Silverhair asked, puzzled.

'Since the last birth. That whining Bull-calf who's always under my feet—'

'Croptail.'

'Too long . . .'

Mammoths do not have clocks, or wrist-watches, or calendars; they do not count out the time in arbitrary packages of seconds and days and years, as humans do. But nevertheless the mammoths know time, on a deep level within themselves. They can measure the slow migration of shadows across the land, the turning faces of Arctic poppies, the strength of air currents. So massive are mammoths that they can *feel* the turn of the Earth on its axis, the slow pulse of the seasons as the Earth spins in its stately annual dance, making the sun arc across the sky – and, so deep and long are their memories, they are even aware of the greater cycles of the planet. There is the Great-Year, the twenty-thousand-year nod of the precessing axis of the spinning planet. And the mammoths know even the million-year cycle of the great ice sheets, which lap against the mountains like huge frozen waves.

So Silverhair knew time. She knew how she was embedded in the great hierarchy of Earth's rhythms.

And she knew that Wolfnose was right.

Wolfnose said, 'One infant, and one half-starved calf. It's not enough to keep the Family going, Grassfoot.'

Grassfoot had been the name of Silverhair's mother – Wolfnose's granddaughter – who, when Silverhair was herself still an infant younger than Croptail was now, had died. Calling Silverhair 'Grassfoot' was a mistake Wolfnose had made before.

'I know,' said Silverhair sadly. 'I know, Great-grandmother.' And, tenderly, she tucked more grass into the old Cow's trembling mouth.

After a time Owlheart came forward. Her huge head loomed over Silverhair, so close that the Matriarch's wiry hair brushed Silverhair's brow. She pulled Silverhair away from Wolfnose.

'I know you're no fool, child,' rumbled Owlheart. 'Sometimes I think you're the smartest, the best of us all.'

Silverhair was startled; she'd never been spoken to like that before.

'But,' the Matriarch went on, 'I want you to understand that there is nowhere so important for you to be, right now, as *here*, at the time of this, our first new birth for many seasons. Never mind headlands. Never mind plausible young Bulls, even. Do you know *why* you must be here?'

'To help my sister.'

The Matriarch shook her great head. 'More than that. *You must learn*. Soon you will be ready for oestrus, ready for a calf of your own. And that calf will depend on you – for its whole life, at first, and later, for the lore and wisdom you can teach it. We don't come into the world fully made, like the birds and the mice. We have to learn how to live. And it will be up to you to teach your calf. There is no greater responsibility. But you cannot teach if you do not learn yourself.' Owlheart stepped back. 'And if you do not learn, you will never become the great Matriarch I think you could be.'

At that, Silverhair's mouth dropped open, and her pink tongue rolled out with surprise. 'Me? A Matriarch?'

It was the most ridiculous thing she had ever heard.

But Owlheart held her gaze. 'It is your destiny, child,' she said sadly. 'Don't you know that yet?'

Chapter Three

THE WALK SOUTH

Mammoths sleep for only a few hours at a time. During the long nights of winter – and during the Arctic summer, when the sun never sets – they sleep not to a fixed pattern but whenever they feel the need.

So, when Silverhair woke, the Moon was still high in the sky, bathing the frozen land in blue light. But soon the short spring day would return. She heard a snow bunting call – a herald of spring – and a raven croaked by overhead.

Silverhair remembered the great mystery she had confronted, and – despite the new calf, despite Owlheart's rumblings – her curiosity was like a pull on her tail, dragging her south again.

Lop-ear was a little way away from the Family, digging in a patch of snow for frozen grass. Silverhair shook frost from her outer guard hair and went to him.

For fear of disturbing the others she silently wrapped her trunk around his and tugged. At first he was reluctant to move; Bull or not, he didn't have quite the powerful streak of curiosity that motivated Silverhair. But after a few heartbeats he let Silverhair lead him away.

Lop-ear spoke with high-pitched chirrups of his trunk that he knew would not carry back to the Family. 'Look at Owlheart.'

Silverhair turned to look back at the Family. She could see the massive dark forms of Owlheart and Wolfnose looming protectively over Foxeye and her new calf. And she could see Owlheart's eyes, like chips of ice in that huge brown head: an unblinking gaze, fixed on her.

'They don't call her Owlheart for nothing,' Lop-ear murmured.

Silverhair shivered. She remembered Owlheart's admonitions; she should stay and spend time with her sister and the calf. But the pull of curiosity in her was too strong. She knew she had to go and explore what she had found on that remote coast.

So she turned away, and the two of them walked on, heading south.

There was ice everywhere, beneath the starry sky. The ridged ice and snow drifts seemed to flow smoothly under their feet.

Silverhair walked steadily and evenly. Her bulk was dark and huge, herself and Lop-ear the only moving things in all this world of white and blue and black. Her walk was a sway of liquid grace, her head nodding with each step, her trunk swaying before her, its great weight obvious. And when she ran, her footsteps were firm, her powerful legs remaining stiff beneath her great weight, her feet swelling slightly as they absorbed her bulk.

They battled through a storm.

The snow and fog swirled around them, matting their hair with freezing moisture, at times making it impossible for them to see more than a few paces ahead. But Silverhair knew this was the last defiant bellow of the dying winter, and she kept her head down and used her bulk to drive herself forward across a tundra that was like a frozen ocean.

And they walked by night, when the only light came from the Moon, which cast a glittering purple glow on the fields of ice and snow. At such times the world was utterly still and silent, save for their own breathing.

To a watching human Silverhair would have looked something like an Asian elephant – but coated with the long, dark-brown hair of a musk ox – round and solid and dark and massive, looking as if she had sprouted from the unforgiving Earth itself.

From the ground under her tree-trunk legs to the top of her broad shoulders – as a human would have measured her – Silverhair was seven feet tall. She was fifteen years old. She could expect to continue growing until she was twenty-five or thirty, until she reached the height of eight or nine feet attained by Owlheart, the Matriarch of the Family. But at that she would be dwarfed by the biggest of the Bulls – like crusty old Eggtusk, who stood all of eleven feet tall at the shoulder.

Her head was large, with a high dome on her crown. Her face, with its long jaw, was surprisingly graceful. Her shoulders had a high, distinctive hump, behind which her back sloped markedly from front to rear – unlike the horizontal line of an elephant's back.

Her body was a machine designed to combat the cold.

The layer of fat under her skin – thick as a human forearm – had kept her warm through the lightless depths of the Arctic winter. Her ears and tail were small, for those thin, exposed organs would otherwise have been at risk from frostbite – but the long hairs which extended from her fleshy tail would let it serve as an effective fly-swat in the mosquito-ridden months of the short summer. There was even a small flap of skin beneath her tail, to seal her anus from the cold.

Her ears had an oddly human shape. Her eyes, too, were small like a human's, and buried deep in a nest of wrinkled skin, shielded from the worst of the weather by thick lashes.

Her tusks were six feet long. Sprouting from their deep sockets at the front of her face, they twisted before her in a loose spiral, their tips almost touching before her. The undersides of both her tusks were worn, for she used them to strip bark and dig up plants – and, in the depths of winter, they served as a snow plough to dig out vegetation for feeding, or even as an ice-breaker to expose water to drink in frozen ponds. The bluish ivory of the tusks was finely textured, with growth rings that mapped her age.

Her trunk, six feet long, served her as her nose, her hand and arm, and was her main feeding apparatus. It was a tube of flesh packed with tiny muscles, capable of movement in any direction, even contraction and extension like a telescope. It had two finger-like extensions at its tip, for manipulating grass and other small objects. As it worked, the trunk's surface folded and wrinkled, betraying the complexity of its structure.

A heavy coat of fur covered her body.

Over a fine downy underwool, her guard hairs were long, coarse and thick, springy and transparent – more like lengths of fishing line than human hair. The hair on her head was just a few inches long. But it hung down in a long fringe under her chin and neck, and at the sides of her trunk. From her flanks and belly hung a skirt of guard hair almost three feet long, giving her something of the look of a Tibetan yak.

Her coat was dark orange-brown, like a musk ox's. And, in a broad cap between the eyes, there lay the patch of snow-white fur that had given Silverhair her name.

Silverhair was *mammuthus primigenius*: a woolly mammoth.

Ten thousand years before, creatures like Silverhair had populated the fringe of the retreating northern ice caps – right around the planet, through Asia from the Baltic to the Pacific, across North America from Alaska to Labrador. But those days were gone.

The isolation of this remote island, off the northern coast of Siberia, had saved Silverhair and her ancestors from the extinction which had washed over the planet, claiming her cousins and many other large animals.

But now the mammoths were trapped here, on the Island.

And Silverhair and her Family were the last of her kind, the last in all the world.

The short days and long nights wore away.

Silverhair and Lop-ear took time to care for their skin. They scratched against an outcropping of rock, luxuriantly dislodging the grasses and dirt which had become stuck in the crevices of their skin and under their hair. They used a patch of dusty, dried-out soil to powder their skin and force out parasites.

Under her thick hair, Silverhair's skin would have looked rough and callused. But it was very sensitive. Under a tough, horny outer layer there were receptors so sensitive she could pinpoint an annoying insect, and brush it off with a precise flick of her trunk or swish of her tail – or even crush it with one focused ripple of her skin.

Nevertheless Silverhair looked forward to the summer, when open puddles of water would be available, and she would be able to wallow comfortably in mud, cooling and washing out ticks and fleas and lice.

'. . . I wonder if Owlheart guessed where we were going?' Lop-ear was saying as he scratched. 'Did you see her talking to Eggtusk?'

'No. But after that lecture I'm surprised she's letting me out of the sight of the calf.'

Lop-ear raised his trunk to sniff at the frosty air. 'She was right. Raising the young is the most important thing of all. But she's obviously making an exception for you.'

'Why?'

'Perhaps because – to Owlheart – this may be more important than anything else you can do – even more important than learning about calves.' Lop-ear rested his trunk on his tusks. 'Owlheart is wise,' he said. 'She listens with more than ears. She listens with her heart and mind. That's why she's Matriarch.'

'And why,' said Silverhair miserably, 'I could never be Matriarch, if I live until the Earth spins itself to dust.' She told Lop-ear what Owlheart had said: that it was her destiny to be Matriarch.

He said, 'She's probably right. There aren't too many candidates.'

'Foxeye—'

'Your sister is a fine mother. But she's weak, Silverhair. You know that. Other than that, there is only Snagtooth.'

Silverhair's hair bristled. 'I would leave the Family if *she* were ever Matriarch. She's mean-spirited, vindictive . . .'

'Then who else is there?'

When she thought it through like that, he was, of course, right. His logic was relentless. But it was all utterly depressing.

'I don't *want* to be a Matriarch,' she said miserably. 'I don't want all that responsibility.'

'Perhaps you really do have the spirit of Longtusk inside you.'

'That's ridiculous,' she said. But she was pleased to hear him say it.

Lop-ear lifted his trunk and rubbed her snow-white scalp

with affection, a gentle touch that thrilled her. 'Like Longtusk, you're a wanderer,' said Lop-ear. 'Perhaps you too could lead us to places no one else could even dream of. And, like Longtusk, you're perverse. After all, Longtusk had to fight to win the command of his Family, didn't he? The story goes the other Bulls all but killed him, rather than accept his orders.'

'But I don't want to fight anybody.'

'Maybe not. But you fight yourself, Silverhair. How typical it is of you that you should choose to model yourself on the one Cycle hero who you could never be, Longtusk the Bull!'

He was right.

In all the great tundra of time reflected in the Cycle, there is only one Bull hero: Longtusk.

When the world warmed, and the ice fell back into the north, the Lost – the mammoths' only true enemy – had come pushing into the mammoth tundra from the south, butchering and murdering. All over the planet mammoths had died, Families and Clans falling together.

. . . All, that is, save the Family of Longtusk: for Longtusk had somehow brought his people across the cold waters here, to the Island. Nobody knew how he had done this: some said he had flown like a bird, carrying his Family on his mighty back; some said he stamped his mighty foot and caused the sea to roar from the ground. At any rate, the Lost had never followed, and the mammoths had been safe.

But Longtusk had given his life . . .

They found a deep puddle with only a thin layer of ice on top. Lop-ear broke through this easily with his tusk, and they plunged their trunks into the water. When Lop-ear had lifted a trunkful he closed his trunk by clenching its fingers, lifted the end and curled it into his mouth. Then he tilted his head back, opened his trunk and let the water gush into his mouth, a delicious and cooling stream.

They soon drained the puddle. But it was a rare treat: standing water had been scarce this winter, and the Family was counting on an early spring thaw. Mammoths need much fresh water each day. They can eat snow, but have to sacrifice precious body heat to melt it.

'Of course,' said Lop-ear, 'even if you were to become Matriarch, I'm not at all sure where you *could* lead us.'

'What do you mean?'

He led her to a patch of frost overlying harder, older ice. He picked up a twig with his trunk and began to scrape at the frost.

'Here is the Island,' he said. It was a rough oval. 'It is surrounded by sea, which we can't cross. To the north there are the Mountains at the End of the World. And to the south, here is the spruce forest.' More scratchings.

Silverhair watched him, baffled. 'What are you doing?'

He looked up. 'I'm—' There was no word for it. 'Imagine you're a bird,' he said at last. 'A guillemot, flying high over the Island.'

'But I'm not a bird.'

'In Kilukpuk's name, Silverhair, if you can imagine yourself as Longtusk you can surely stretch your mind that far!'

She stretched out her ears and spun, pretending to wheel like a bird. 'Look at me! Caw! Caw!'

'All right, Silverhair the gull. Now, you're looking down at the Island. You see it sitting in the middle of the sea, like a lump of dung in a pond. Yes?'

'Yes . . .'

'Look – now!' With his trunk, he pointed to the frost scrapings he had made.

And – looking down as if she were a mammoth-gull, concentrating hard – for a heartbeat, yes, she could see the Island, see it through his scrapings, just as if she really was a gull, balanced on the winds high above.

To Silverhair, the simple drawing was a kind of magic; she had never seen anything like it.

'Every time the Earth spins around the sun the summer is a little longer, the winter a little less harsh. And the forest encroaches a little more on the tundra.' Absently Lop-ear dug in the soil with his tusks, burrowed with his trunk and produced a scraping of grass. 'You know, Wolfnose remembers a time – when she was only a calf herself – when the spruce forest was just a few straggling saplings clinging to the coast. And *now* look how far it has spread.' With his twig, he pointed to the middle of the Island. 'You see? We are contained in this strip of the Island, between forest and mountains, like a calf that has fallen in a mud hole. And the strip is narrowing.'

'So what do we do?'

'I don't know. This Island is all we have. We have absolutely nowhere else to go.'

She admired Lop-ear's unusual mind, the clarity and depth of thinking he was capable of. But his logic was chilling. 'It can't be true,' she said. 'What about the Sky Steppe?'

Lop-ear said, 'Do you really believe that?'

Silverhair was scandalised. 'Lop-ear, it's in the *Cycle*.'

The Cycle contains tales of a mysterious steppe which floats in the sky, where – the story goes – mammoths will one day roam free.

But Lop-ear was growling. 'Look – we can know the past because we remember it, and we can tell it to our calves, who remember it in turn . . . Through the Cycle, and the memories of our mothers, we can "remember" all the way back to Kilukpuk's Swamp. That's all sensible. But as to the future—' He tossed his twig in the air. 'We can no more know the future than we can say how that twig will fall.'

The stick rattled to the bone-hard ground, out of her sight.

'And besides,' he said, 'there might soon be nobody to go to the Sky Steppe anyhow.'

'What do you mean?'

He looked at her mournfully. 'Think about it. When was the last time you heard a contact rumble from my bachelor herd – or any other Family, come to that? How many mammoths have we seen on this trek? We haven't even found footprints or fresh dung—'

The thought was chilling; she turned away from it. 'You think too much.'

'I wish I could stop,' he said quietly.

They moved on, through cloudy day and Moonlit night.

They came to a place they knew was good for salty soil. It was frozen over, but they set to scraping at the ice with their tusks until they had exposed some of the bone-hard soil. Then they dug out a little and tucked it into their mouths; it was dry and dusty, but it contained salt and other minerals otherwise missing from the mammoths' diet.

And, nearby, under a thin layer of hoar frost, they found a heap of mammoth dung. It was reasonably fresh, and hope briefly lifted; perhaps other Families were, after all, close.

But then Silverhair recognised the dung's sharp scent. 'Why, it's mine,' she said. 'I must have come this way before.'

Lop-ear broke open the pat of dung – it wasn't quite frozen in the centre – and began to lift chunks of it to his mouth. Mammoths will eat a little dung to sustain the colonies of bacteria that live in their guts, which help them digest grasses.

'Maybe our luck is changing, even so,' he said, around a mouthful of soil and dung.

'How?'

'Look up.'

She did so, and saw a curtain of light streaks spread across the sky – mostly yellow and crimson, fading to black, but here and there tinged with green. It extended from the horizon, all the way up the sky, almost to the zenith over their heads. The curtain rippled gently, like the guard hairs that dangle from the belly of a mammoth.

It was an aurora.

Mammoths believe the aurora is made up of the spirits of every mammoth who has ever lived, brought to life again by a wind from the sun, so joyous they dance at the very top of the air.

Lop-ear said, 'What do you think? Is Longtusk up there somewhere, looking down on us? Do you think he's come to guide our way?'

And indeed, the ghostly light of the aurora had made the Moonlit landscape glow green and blue, almost as brightly as day.

With uplifted hearts, they set off once more.

After days of walking they climbed a shallow ridge which gave them a view of the Island's south coast, and Silverhair could see the pale blue-white gleam of pack ice on the sea. But between the two mammoths and the coast, lying over the land like a layer of guard hair, was the spruce forest. The first isolated, straggling trees were already close.

The two mammoths skirted the darker depths of the forest, staying at the northern fringe where only a few scattered, stunted trees encroached on the rocky tundra, ancient plants that grew no higher than their own bellies. It was well known that wolves inhabited the deeper forest. It was unlikely that even a pack would take on two full-grown mammoths, but inside the denser parts of the forest movement would be difficult, and it would be foolish to offer the wily predators any opportunity.

The only sound was the crunch of ice beneath their feet, the hiss of breath in their trunks, and the low moan of the wind in the trees. In the branches of a dwarf spruce a solitary capercaillie sat, unperturbed, eyeing them as they passed.

Night was falling by the time they reached the headland.

The sea opened up before them, flat and calm. A fringe of fast ice pushed out from the land, hard and glistening. Further out the sea ice was littered with trapped icebergs, sculptured mountains of ice that glowed green and blue. And Silverhair could see the rope of water that cut off the Island from the Mainland – which was, she saw, still shrouded by storm clouds, hiding the glittering and mysterious array of lights that clustered there.

As the sun waned, the colours faded to an ice-blue twilight. The air grew colder, and the sea water steamed.

It was a bleak, frozen scene. But there was life here. More seabirds were arriving from the south, fulmars and black guillemots, and they had begun their elaborate courtship in the pink, watery sunshine. Seals slid through the open water, snorting when they broke the surface.

Beneath the headland there was a valley which descended to the rocky southern coast. Silverhair and Lop-ear clambered down this valley now.

Between the walls of the valley, nothing moved save an occasional swirl of dry snow crystals lifted by the wind. The mountainside here had been blown almost clear of snow, and in the shade the rock was covered by a treacherous glaze of ice. The mammoths' broad feet gripped the ground well; the round soles were thickened into ridges for that purpose. But even so Silverhair's feet slid out from under her, and she barely managed to keep from stumbling. Once she found herself teetering on the edge of a sheet drop into a snow-filled chasm.

Surrounded by these huge walls of ice and rock, Silverhair

received an unwelcome perspective on the smallness and frailty of even a mammoth's life.

At last they reached the beach. It was growing dark, and they decided to wait out the long night here.

The beach was a strange place, where neither of them felt comfortable.

For one thing it was noisy, compared to the thick stillness of the Arctic nights they were used to: there was the continual lapping of the sea at the shingle, the crunching of stones beneath their shifting feet, the snapping and groaning of the sea ice as it rose and fell in response to the oily surges of the water beneath. There was no food to be had here, for this eroded, shifting place was neither land nor sea. It was even considered a waste to pass dung here, for it would be merely washed away to sea rather than enrich the land.

They endured a long, uncomfortable night of broken sleep.

The dawn, when at last it came, was clear. The sky turned an intense blue, and the sea ice was so white that the horizon was a firm line. And as the sunrise itself approached, a shaft of deep-red light shot suddenly straight up, piercing the blue. Silverhair looked out over the sea ice, and saw that, thanks to a mirage effect, the distant pack ice seemed to be lifting into the sky, illusory towers rising and falling in the heat from the sun. And when the sun rose a little higher she saw a ghostly companion rise with it, a halo scattered by ice crystals in the air.

Lop-ear, impulsively, ran to the water's edge. Breaking the thin ice there, he waded in until his legs were immersed up to his hips, and his belly hair was soaked and floating loosely on the surface.

He looked back at Silverhair. 'Come on. What are you waiting for?'

Silverhair took a hesitant step forward. She dipped one foot in the water, and steeled herself to go further.

Silverhair had an abiding dread of deep water. As a small calf, she had almost fallen into a fast-flowing glacier runoff stream. She had been washed down the stream, bobbing like a piece of rotten wood, her squeals all but drowned out by the rush of water. Only the fast brain and strong trunk of Wolfnose had saved her from being dashed against the rocks, or drowned.

Lop-ear waded clumsily back towards her; he splashed her, and the water droplets were icy. 'I'm sorry,' he said. 'I forgot. That was stupid of me.'

'It's all right. I'm just being foolish.'

Lop-ear grunted. 'There's nothing foolish about learning to avoid danger.' He quoted the Cycle. '*The wolf's first bite is its responsibility. Its second is yours.* I'm being selfish—'

'No.' And Silverhair waded forward deliberately, leading the way into the ocean.

The water immediately soaked through the hair over her legs. Close to freezing, its cold penetrated to her skin. Her hair, waving like seaweed around her belly, impeded her progress. The sheets of landfast ice crackled around her legs and chest.

Lop-ear stopped her. 'That's far enough,' he said. 'Now—'

Awkwardly he knelt down, so his chest was immersed. Then he dipped his head; soon the water was lapping over his eyes and forehead.

He lifted his head in a great spray, and she could see frost forming on his hair and eyelashes. He said, 'Did you hear me?'

With great reluctance, she dropped her head so that her trunk and right ear were immersed in the icy water. Lop-ear extended his trunk underwater and emitted a series of strange calls: deep-toned whistles and bleats, mixed with higher-pitched squeaks and squeals.

'What are you doing?'

'Calling our Cousins. The Calves of Siros. Don't you know your Cycle? The *sea cows*, Silverhair.'

She snorted. 'But the sea cows all died lifetimes ago. The Lost hunted them even harder than they hunted us. That's what the Cycle says—'

'The Cycle isn't always right.'

'Have you ever *seen* a sea cow?'

'No,' he said. 'But I've never seen the back of my own head either. Doesn't mean to say it doesn't exist.' And he thrust his trunk back into the sea and continued his plaintive call.

Reluctantly she ducked her ear back under the water.

The sea had its own huge, hollow noises, like an immense empty cavern. She heard the voices of seals: birdlike chirrups, long swooping whistles, and short popping cries that the seals bounced off the ice sheets above them, using the echoes to seek out their air holes. Then, deeper and more remote, there were the groans of whales, and still deeper calls which might come from half the world away . . .

And – briefly – there was a series of low whistles, interspersed with high-pitched squeaks and squeals.

But the sound died away.

They lifted their heads out of the water. They looked at each other.

'It was probably only an echo,' she said. 'Some undersea cliff.'

'I know. There's nothing there. But wouldn't it have been wonderful *if*—'

'Come on. Let's go and get warm.'

They turned and splashed their way out of the water. Silverhair shook her head to rid it of the frost that was forming. To get their blood flowing through their chilled skin once more, they played: they chased each other across the shingle, mock-wrestled with their trunks, and gambolled like calves.

Silverhair looked back once, at the place where they had called to the sea cows.

Far out in the Channel she thought she could see something surfacing: huge, black, sleek. But then it was gone.

It was probably just a trick of the light.

Chapter Four

THE MONSTER OF THE ICE FLOE

When they were warm they continued along the beach, in search of the peculiar creatures Silverhair had spotted.

Hundreds of guillemots were arriving on the cliffs above them. This first sign of the summer's burst of fecundity seemed incongruous on such a bitterly cold morning; in fact, the nesting ledges were still covered in snow and ice. But the seabirds had to start early if they were to complete their breeding cycle before, all too soon, the snow of winter returned. And so the birds clung to the cliffs and fought over the prime nesting sites. So intense were these battles, Silverhair saw, that two birds, locked together beak to bloody beak, fell from the high cliffs and dashed themselves against the sea ice below.

Fast as a spray of blown snow an Arctic fox darted forward and grabbed both birds, killing them immediately. The fox buried his catch in the ice, and returned to the foot of the nesting cliff in search of more pickings.

From a snow bank high on the cliff a female polar bear, her fur yellow-white, pushed her way out of her den. She yawned and stretched, and Silverhair wondered if this was the bear she had seen before.

The bear clambered back up to her den, and sat by the entrance. After a time a cub appeared – small, dumpy and dazzling white – and greeted the world with terrified squeaks. A second cub emerged, then a third. The mother walked confidently down the steep cliff towards the sea, while the cubs looked on with trepidation. At last two of the cubs followed her, gingerly, sliding backwards, their claws clutching the snow. The other stayed in the den entrance and cried so loudly its mother returned with the others, and she suckled all three in the sun. Then the bear walked steadily down to the sea ice – in search of her first meal since the autumn – and her cubs clumsily followed.

The mammoths walked around a rocky spur, and came to the Nest of Straight Lines.

Lop-ear slowed, his eyes wide, his trunk held up in the air, his good ear cocked, alert for danger.

Silverhair was trembling, for this was an unnatural place. But still, she said: 'We have to go on. The strange ice floe, whatever it was, must have come to rest further on than this. Come on.'

And, without allowing herself to hesitate, she set off along the beach. After a few heartbeats she heard Lop-ear's heavy steps crackling on the shingle as he followed.

In this mysterious place, set back from the beach, a series of blocky shapes huddled against the cliff. They were dark and angular, each of them much larger even than a mammoth. The great blocks were hollowed out. Holes gaped in their sides and tops, allowing in the low sunlight; but there was no movement within.

Lop-ear said, 'Those things look like skulls to me.'

Looking again, she saw that he was right: *skulls*, but with eye sockets and gaping mouths made out of straight lines, and big enough for a mammoth to climb inside.

'They must be the skulls of giants, then,' she said.

And the most horrific aspect of the place was that the whole of it was constructed of hard, straight lines. It was the lines which had earned the place its mammoth name, for, aside from the horizon line and the trunks of trees, there are few long straight lines in nature.

In the centre of the Nest there was a great stalk: like the trunk of a tree, but not solid, made of sticks and spars through which Silverhair could see the pale dawn sky. And at the top of the stalk there was a series of big round shells, like the petals of a flower – but much bigger, so big they looked as if a mammoth could clamber inside.

The mammoths peered up at the assemblage of brooding forms, dwarfed.

'Perhaps those things up there are the ears of the giants who lived here,' said Lop-ear, awed.

'But what *happened* to the giants?'

'You know what Eggtusk says.'

'What?'

'That this place has nothing to do with giants,' he said.

'Then what?'

'*Lost*,' said Lop-ear. 'The Lost made this.'

And, as he spoke the name of the mammoths' most dread enemy of the past, it was Silverhair's turn to shiver.

By unspoken consent, they hurried on.

A flat sheet, lying on the shingle, briefly caught Silverhair's eye. It looked at first like a broken sheet of ice, but, as she came closer, she saw that it was made of wood – though she knew of no tree which produced such huge, straight-edged branches.

There were markings on the sheet.

She slowed, studying the markings. The patterns reminded

her oddly of the scrapings Lop-ear had made in the frost. There was a splash of yellow, almost like a flower – or like a star, cupped in a crescent Moon. And beneath it, a collection of lines and curves that had no meaning for her:

USSR

AIR FORCE

SECURE AREA

ENTRANCE PROHIBITED

She wanted to ask Lop-ear about it; perhaps he would understand. But he had already hurried ahead, and she didn't want to linger here, alone in this unnatural place; she ran to catch him up.

With the Nest of Straight Lines behind them, they approached the half-frozen sea.

'What I saw must have been about here,' said Silverhair, trying to think.

Lop-ear looked around and raised his trunk. 'I can't smell anything.'

The two mammoths walked a little way on to the ice, which squeaked and crackled under them. The ice that clung closest to the shore, where the sea was frozen all the way to the bottom, was called landfast ice. It formed in protected bays, or else drifted in from the sea. Its width varied depending on how deep the water was. Later in the summer the landfast ice would break free and melt, or drift away with the pack ice.

The pack ice was the frozen surface of the deeper ocean. It was a blue-white sheet crumpled into pressure ridges, like lines of sand dunes sculpted in white. Further away from the land Silverhair could see black lines carved in the ice: leads, cracks exposing open water between the loose mass of floes. As the spring wore on the leads would extend in towards the coast, splitting off the ice floes. The floes would break up, or be washed out to open sea by the powerful current which ran between the Mainland and the Island.

Dark clouds hung over the open Channel, that forbidding stretch of black water; the clouds formed from the steam rising from the water.

And, on a floe far from the land, she made out a black, unmoving shape.

She trumpeted in triumph. Gulls, startled awake, cawed in response.

'There!' she cried. 'Do you see it?'

Lop-ear, patiently, stared where she did. 'I don't see a thing. Just pressure ridges, and shadows . . . *Oh*.'

'You do see it! You do! That's what I saw, floating in the sea – and now it's on the ice.'

It might have been the size of a mammoth, she supposed – but a mammoth lying inert on the floe. All Silverhair's fear had evaporated like hoar frost, so great was her gladness at rediscovering the strange object. 'Come on.' And she set out across the landfast ice.

Reluctantly, Lop-ear followed.

As they moved away from the shore, the quality of the sound changed. The soft lapping of the sea was gone, and the ice creaked and groaned as it shifted on the sea, a deep rumble like the call of a mammoth.

The pressure ridges were high here, frozen waves that came almost up to her shoulder. The ridges were topped by blue ice, scoured clean by the wind, and soft snow lay in the hollows between them. The ridges were difficult to scramble over, so Silverhair found a lead and walked along at the edge of the water, where the ice was flatter.

Frost-smoke, sparkling in the sunlight, rose from the black, oily water.

On one floe she found the grisly site of a polar bear's kill. It was a seal's breathing hole, iced over and tinged with blood. She could see a bloodstained area of ice where the bear must have dragged the seal and devoured it. And there was a hollowed-out area of snow near a pressure ridge, marked by black excrement, where the bear had probably slept after its bloody feast.

The wind picked up. Ice crystals swirled around her. When she looked up at the sun, she saw there was a halo around it. She knew she must be careful, for that was a sign the sea ice might break up.

She came to a place where the pressure ridges towered over her. Surrounded by the ridges, all she could see were the neighbouring hummocks and the sky above.

She struggled to the top of a crag of ice.

From here she could see the tops of the other ridges, and the narrow valleys that separated them. They looked as if they had been scraped into this ice surface by some gigantic tusk.

And she realised that she had walked further out to sea than she had imagined, for she found herself staring up at an ice-berg.

It was a wedge-shaped block trapped in the pack ice. She saw how its base had been sculpted into great smooth columns by the water that lapped there, and by the scouring of wind-blown particles of ice and snow. The sunlight flooded the berg with blue light, a blueness that seemed to shine from within the body of the translucent ice.

Further from the shore she saw many giant bergs, frozen in, standing stark and majestic all across the sea ice. The ice between the bergs was smooth and flat. Older bergs, sil-houetted in the low light, were wind-sculpted and melted, some of them carved into spires, arches, pinnacles, caves and other fantastic shapes. Perhaps they would not survive another summer. She could see that some of the bergs had shattered into smaller pieces, and here and there she made out growlers, the hard, compact cores of melted bergs, made of compressed, greenish ice, polished smooth by the waves.

In the light of the low sun, the colours of the bergs varied from white to blue, pink and purple, even a rich muddy brown, strange-shaped scraps littering the pack ice.

And from this vantage, Silverhair saw the strange object she had come so far to find.

Dark and mysterious, the thing rested on a floe that had all but broken away from the main mass of pack ice. Only a neck of ice, ten or eleven paces wide, still connected the floe to the land.

She scrambled down the ridge to the edge of the floe. Then she hesitated, looking down with trepidation at the narrow ice bridge, and the unyielding blackness of the water below. Lop-ear came to join her.

'It's quite wide,' she said uncertainly. She took a step forward, near the centre of the bridge, and pushed at the ice with her lead foot. It creaked and bowed, meltwater pooling under her foot, but it held. 'If I keep away from the edges it should be safe.'

'Silverhair, that's terribly dangerous.'

'We've come this far—'

And without letting herself think about it any further, she stepped forward on to the bridge.

One step, then another: avoiding the rotten ice, testing every pace, she worked her way steadily across the bridge.

The water lapped only a few paces to either side of her.

At last she arrived on the floe. The ice here, though bowing a little, was relatively solid. There were even some pressure ridges, one or two of them as tall as she was.

She turned and looked back to Lop-ear. He was a compact, dark shape on a broad sheet of blue-white ice, and he seemed a long way away.

She raised her trunk and trumpeted bravely, 'Don't follow me. The bridge is fragile.'

'Come back as soon as you can, Silverhair.'

'I will.'

She turned and, with caution, made her way across the floe.

The mysterious object was, she supposed, about the size of a large adult mammoth. Overall it looked something like a huge, stretched-out eggshell. It was flat at one end, and tusk-sharp at the other, and hollow inside. But she could see that the bottom of it was smashed to pieces, perhaps by a collision with the ice.

It certainly wasn't made of ice.

She reached out a tentative trunk-finger, and stroked its surface.

She snatched back her trunk, shocked. It was *wood*: covered by some hard, shining coat – a coat that masked its smell – but wood nonetheless.

The short hairs on her scalp prickled. Something about this thing – perhaps the short, sharp lines of its construction – reminded her unpleasantly of the Nest of Straight Lines.

There was a cracking sound.

'Silverhair!' Lop-ear's voice sounded disturbingly remote.

She spun around and, in the light of the already setting sun, she saw two things simultaneously.

The narrow ice bridge back to the pack ice had collapsed, stranding her here.

And there was a monster on the ice floe.

The monster seemed to have stepped from behind a pressure

ridge, where it had been hidden from her view – and she from its. She couldn't understand how it had got so close; it was as if it had no scent. It was smaller than she was – much smaller. It was, perhaps, about the size of a small seal. It had four legs. It was standing on its hind legs, like a seal balancing on its tail.

But this was no seal.

For its legs were long: longer, in proportion, even than a mammoth's. It was skinny – surely it could not withstand the cold with so little fat to insulate it – and it didn't have any fur, not even on its shiny, hairless, skull-like head. In fact it seemed to have nothing to protect it but a loose-fitting outer skin.

Its ears were small, and startlingly like a mammoth's. Its eyes were set at the front of its head, like a wolf's – a predator's eyes, the better to hunt with. And now those binocular eyes were fixed on Silverhair, in fear or calculation.

It was clutching things in its forelegs. In one paw it held something shiny, like a shard of ice. In the other, there was something soft that dripped blood. It was the liver of a walrus, she recognised. And there was blood all around the monster's small mouth.

A child of Aglu, then. And perhaps strangest of all that eerie lack of any scent.

She must show no fear. What would Longtusk have done in such a situation?

She lowered her head so her tusks would not seem a threat, and she spoke to the creature. 'I am called Silverhair,' she said. 'And you—'

Its predator's eyes were wide, its gaze fixed on her, its small, hairless face wreathed in steam. And there was frost on its shining dome of a head. It was a male, she decided, for she could see no sign of dugs.

'I will call you Skin-of-Ice,' she said.

She took a step towards the creature, meaning to touch him

with her trunk, as mammoths will when they meet; perhaps she would go through the greeting ritual with him.

But he cried out. He raised the glittering, sharp thing in his paw, and backed away.

The wind picked up, abruptly, and ice crystals whirled around her face. The floe rocked, and she stumbled.

When she looked again, the monster had gone.

She caught one last glimpse of him, hopping nimbly across the widening leads, heading for the shore far from Silverhair and Lop-ear.

The wind began to blow more strongly through the Channel. The sea became choppy, and as it drifted through the Channel the ice floe began to break up. Soon Silverhair found herself stranded in a mass of loose ice that was drifting rapidly eastwards.

Suddenly she was in peril.

But now Lop-ear was calling her, with a deep rumble that easily crossed the ice and water to her. 'This way! This way!'

She saw that a smaller floe had nudged alongside the floe she rode. It was even more fragile than the one she was on – but it was closer to the shore.

Not allowing herself to hesitate, she marched briskly across the narrow lead to the smaller floe.

Behind her the ice at the floe's edge crumbled into fragments.

This floe, much smaller than the first, was spinning slowly, and heaving from side to side in the heavy swell as the current swept it along. Then another floe came bumping alongside with a crunch of smashing ice; she hurried forward, and found herself a little closer again to land.

So she worked her way, floe by floe, across the ice, following a complex path that she hoped would lead her to the shore.

At the edge of one floe, a herd of walrus were gambolling among the loose ice. They completely ignored her. It was a mixed group, mothers with calves of various ages, and one massive male with long curved tusks protruding from his small face. Some of the walrus had their tusks hooked to the edge of the ice as they rested, to save themselves from sinking as they slept. The stink was almost overpowering, for it seemed they had been defecating on the same floe all winter. The walrus scratched hoar-frost from their bodies with surprisingly gentle flippers, and occasionally turned over in a great heap of pinkish blubbery flesh, their long ivory tusks glinting in the sun.

With their warty skin, wide moustaches and tiny heads atop their long, ponderous bodies, Silverhair found it hard to think of the walrus as anything but spectacularly ugly. She wondered sadly if one of this comfortable family had fallen victim to Skin-of-Ice. Perhaps they didn't know about it yet.

Silverhair skirted the walrus carefully.

Her progress was agonising – one step forward, another back – and she lost track of the time she had spent here, inching across the treacherous ice.

Brown mist, blown from over the open water, swirled around her, making it hard to keep to her chosen track. The loose floes spun around, crashed and tilted, and she felt as if the whole world, of ice and sea and land, was in motion. More than once she stepped through rotten ice, and her feet took more dunkings in the water, and the fur on her legs was soon heavy and stiff with ice.

If she couldn't get back to the shore, these separating floes would, eventually, be blown out to sea. There – the Cycle taught – she would suffer death by starvation or thirst – if the floes did not crumble and drown her, and if killer whales did not ram their snouts through the thinning ice to reach her.

But gradually, she realised, she was working her way, floe by floe, step by step, back towards the shore. Lop-ear ran along faithfully, calling out the floes he spotted, evidently determined he would not abandon her.

At last, as she neared the landfast ice and got away from the fastest-flowing water, the swell subsided, and the rolling of the floes became more bearable.

And then she found herself on a hard, unyielding surface.

For a moment she stood there, unable to believe it was over, that she had reached the land. In fact, she felt giddy, so used had she become to standing on a surface that tipped and heaved beneath her. But Lop-ear's trunk was soon over her head, touching her mouth and cooing reassurance.

With relief, she trotted away from the ice's edge.

She turned and saw the floe that had so nearly carried her to her death. There was the anonymous hulk of distorted wood. And there, just visible as black dots on the ice, were the droppings she had made as she had circled the shrinking floe.

But now frost-smoke and the mist off the sea closed around the floe, and it was carried away to invisibility.

Chapter Five

THE TUSK

The Family was a small, bulky knot in the landscape, dark on dark. But Silverhair could hear the mammoths' rumbles and chirrups, kindly or complaining in turn; she could feel the deep sound passing through the frozen earth as those great feet lumbered back and forth; and she could smell the welcoming smell of wet mammoth fur, a rich stink that carried on the wind. She could even smell the moist, slightly stale aroma of the milk her sister was producing for her new calf.

And as they approached the Family, Silverhair saw that the Matriarch was preparing for a migration.

Owlheart was moving among her charges, gathering and encouraging them with gentle slaps of her trunk. Silverhair's sister, Foxeye, was gathering her calves around her. Foxeye herself looked unsteady on her feet, weakened by the long trial of her pregnancy and the birth. Sunfire, the new baby, stayed close to her mother, nestling in the long hairs of Foxeye's belly. The calf's milk tusks were already budding at her cheeks, white as Arctic flowers. Silverhair heard Foxeye murmuring the ancient tale of Kilukpuk's calves to her, and she remembered how her own mother – when Silverhair wasn't much older than Sunfire was now – had made her swear the ancient Oath of Kilukpuk. And there was little Croptail, scarcely more than an infant himself, his baffled resentment of his new sister visible even from afar.

Snagtooth and Wolfnose stood a little distance away, cropping the sparse, dry grass that protruded through the frost. Neither of them took much part in the proceedings: Snagtooth seemed, as usual, sullen and withdrawn, and Wolfnose, though standing straight and tall, was very still, and Silverhair knew that she was trying to spare her worn-out knees before the long trek that faced her.

And there was stolid old Eggtusk, unmistakable for that bulb of ivory on his tusk, if not for his mighty shoulders. The powerful old Bull stood shoulder to shoulder to Owlheart, supporting everything she said and did.

Silverhair's heart warmed as she looked over her Family, one by one, bedraggled as their dark winter fur blew away from their backs; suddenly the twenty days of her separation from them seemed much longer.

'We must tell them what we saw,' said Silverhair to Lop-ear. 'The strange creature on the floe—'

'No,' said Lop-ear. 'Not now.'

'Why not? Surely Owlheart and Eggtusk will be able to help us make sense of it.'

'They have other things on their minds right now. And besides . . .' He shook his great head, so that rust-brown hair fell over his eyes. 'I have a feeling it isn't something the Matriarch will be glad to hear.'

Silverhair found herself shivering at his words. She knew he had touched on the truth. When she thought back now over the incident with Skin-of-Ice, the ice floe monster, she felt little but dread. But that wasn't logical, she told herself. Everything strange seemed frightening at first; it didn't mean it was necessarily *bad* . . .

They trotted forward and joined the Family.

The greeting ceremony was affectionate but brief, for Owlheart was trying to ensure that everybody's mind was on the migration. But Silverhair, ignoring Lop-ear's advice, approached Owlheart, and told the Matriarch what she had found.

She tried to crystallise the monster for the Matriarch: walking upright on two long legs, strange objects held in the paws of the forelegs, face smeared with the blood of the walrus, helplessly thin, but coated with artificial fur – and, strangest of all, that utter lack of scent.

Owlheart listened, and caressed Silverhair's ear. 'My poor granddaughter,' she rumbled. 'If only you had a little less of Longtusk in you. But perhaps it's as well for all of us that you don't.'

'What do you mean?'

'You must tell nobody else what you saw. Do you understand?'

'But Lop-ear—'

'*Nobody*.'

And the Matriarch trotted away, trunk held high as if to detect danger, towards Eggtusk. They began to speak, a long and serious conversation punctuated by glares at Silverhair.

Silverhair sighed. She didn't know why, but it seemed she was in trouble again.

After a final bout of defecation, a final brief graze, the migration began.

The walk was not easy.

The new calf, Sunfire, was thin and sickly. At the frequent

stops, Silverhair helped Foxeye with simple mammoth medicine. She would place her trunk into the calf's tiny mouth, ensuring she did not choke on her food; and, at rest times, she nudged the baby to her feet, for there was a danger that the infant's weight would press down on her lungs and prevent her breathing.

Wolfnose, too, was having a great deal of difficulty walking. All four of her legs, stiffened with arthritis, seemed as inflexible as tree-trunks as they clumped down on the frozen ground. And several bones in her back were fused into hard, painful units. She was too proud to admit to the pain, still less give in to it. But Wolfnose was clearly able to keep up only a slow pace.

The others helped by huddling her. Eggtusk and the Matriarch herself walked along to either side, helping Wolfnose stay upright, and Lop-ear walked behind her, gently nudging her great thighs to keep her going.

The world was silent around them, empty as a skull. The only sound was the crackle of frost under their feet, the hiss of breath through their long nostrils, and the occasional word of instruction or encouragement from the adults, or complaint from the calves. The land was mostly flat, but here and there they had to clamber over frozen hills, blocks of ice embedded in the ground.

As Silverhair walked, she could picture where she was, imagine the mammoths crawling across the great, empty belly of the Island.

The mammoths' ability to hear the deepest noises of the Earth enables them to do much more than communicate over long distances. Mammoths can *hear* the distinctive voices of the landscape: the growl of breaking waves and cracking ice at a seashore, the low humming of bare sand, the droning of the wind through mountains. All this enables them to build up a complex, three-dimensional map of the world around them, extending to regions far beyond the horizon. They are able to predict the weather – for they can hear the growl of turbulent air in the atmosphere – and even receive warnings about Earth tremors, for the booming bellow of seismic waves as they pass through the planet's rocky heart is the deepest voice of all.

So Silverhair had a kind of map in her head that encompassed the whole of the Island, and even a sense of the roundness of the Earth, spinning and nodding on its endless dance around the sun. Silverhair's mind had deep roots – deeper than any human's – roots that extended into the rocky structure of the world itself.

But her powerful ability to listen to the planet's many voices also made her uncomfortably aware that this was the *only* mammoth group she could sense, right across the Island. She could feel the sweep and extent of the rocky land, and the mammoths were stranded at the centre of this huge, echoing landscape like pebbles thrown on to an ice floe.

She felt distracted, restless, disturbed. Where *was* everybody?

They passed a family of wolves.

The wolves were lying on the ground, huddled against the cold, their white-furred backs turned to the teeth of the wind, their heads tucked into their bellies for warmth. An adult – perhaps a bitch – stood up and glared as Silverhair thudded past.

'Once,' rumbled Wolfnose, eyeing the wolf, 'I saw a mammoth brought down by a wolf pack. Long before any of you were born. He was a calf – a Bull, called Willowleg, for his legs were spindly and weak. The wolves pursued him, despite the efforts of the rest of the Family to keep them off. The wolves are smart. They took it in turns to pick up the running, so they did not tire as Willowleg did.

'At last they cornered him in a crevasse, where the rest of us could not follow. Willowleg got his back to the rock wall and fought. But there were many wolves. First they cut him down, with bites to his legs and hindquarters, and then, at last, they got in a killing bite to the throat. And then they pulled him apart.

'Wolves have Family too,' she said, her old eyes sunk in folds of skin. 'The lead male eats first, then his senior bitches, and any female which is feeding cubs.' She regarded the wide-eyed calves. 'It is the way of things. But be wary of the wolves.'

Silverhair could see the wolf's moist eyes, the gleam of her teeth in the sunlight, and imagined the calculation going on in her sharp-edged mind, the dark legacy of Aglu, brother of Kilukpuk.

Wolfnose's story was a timely warning. Of all of them, for all his greater size and strength compared with Sunfire, Croptail was probably the most vulnerable to predators like the wolves. He could no longer rely on the close protection of Foxeye – she was preoccupied with the new infant, and her instincts were in any event to push the growing Bull away – but he had not yet learned to forage effectively for himself, or to defend himself from the wolves. So Silverhair made sure she always knew where Croptail had got to, and she stopped periodically and raised her trunk, listening and sniffing for signs of danger on the wind.

The days were still cruelly short, but nevertheless lengthening, with the sun's brief arc above the horizon extending with each day that passed. The weather remained clear and bitterly cold. Wind whipped across the empty ground, blowing up particles of ice so small and hard and dry they felt like grit when they got into Silverhair's eyes.

One day, when the sun was at its height and bathing the frosty ground with a spurious gold, Owlheart called a halt. The mammoths dispersed to scrape grass from the hard ground and drop dung.

The calves found the energy to play. Sunfire pestered her older brother, placing her trunk in his mouth to test the grass he was eating, rubbing against him and even collapsing in a heap beside him. At times they chased each other, mounting mock charges and wrestling with their trunks.

Foxeye wearily admonished Croptail to be careful with his sister, but Silverhair knew such play was important in teaching the calves to develop their own abilities – and, most important, to learn about each other, for it was the bond between Family members that was the most important weapon of all in their continued survival. Anyhow, the calves' cheerful play warmed the dispirited adults.

Poor Wolfnose stood stiffly, away from the others, her great legs visibly trembling.

Owlheart called Silverhair, Lop-ear and Snagtooth to her.

Owlheart began digging at the ground. She broke the crusted surface with her tusks and forefeet, scooping the debris out of the way with her trunk. Her left tusk was much more worn than the right: a good deal shorter, and its tip was rounded and grooved. Most mammoths favour their right tusk as their master tusk, but Owlheart, unusually, preferred the left, and that showed in the unevenness of the wear.

'The winter has been dry,' said Owlheart as she dug. 'Perhaps the thaw will come soon, but we are thirsty now. But here, in this place, there is water to be found – liquid, for most of the year. This is a place where the inner warmth of the Earth reaches to the surface, and keeps the water here beneath from freezing, even when the world is as cold as a corpse's belly . . .'

Now, looking around more carefully, Silverhair saw the ground was pitted by a series of shallow craters: pits dug in the ground by mammoths of the past.

'*Remember this place*,' Owlheart said. 'For it is a place of Earth's generous warmth, and water; and it may save your life.'

Silverhair turned, scanning the horizon. She raised her trunk and let the hairs there dangle in the prevailing wind. She studied the sky, and scraped with her tusks at the ground. She let the scents and subtle sounds of the landscape sink into her mind.

She was *remembering*. Even as Owlheart spoke she was adding a new detail, exquisite but perhaps vitally important, to the map of scents and breezes and textures that each mammoth carried in her head.

'Now, help me dig,' said Owlheart.

Silverhair, Lop-ear and Snagtooth stepped forward, took their places around the preliminary hole dug by their Matriarch, and began to work at the ground.

The ground was hard: even to the stone-hard tusks of mammoths, it offered stiff resistance. Save for the occasional peevish complaint by Snagtooth, there was no talking as they worked: only the scrape of tusk and stamp of foot, the hissing of breath through upraised trunks.

They worked through the night, taking breaks in turn.

As the night wore on – and as there was little sign of water, and they became steadily more exhausted – Silverhair had a growing sense of unease.

Owlheart was not a Matriarch who welcomed debate about her decisions. Nevertheless, as Owlheart took a break – standing to pass her dung a little way away from the others – Silverhair summoned up the courage to speak to her.

Owlheart was evidently weary already from her work, and her pink tongue protruded from her mouth.

'You're thirsty,' said Silverhair.

'Yes. A paradox, isn't it – that the work to find water is making me thirstier than ever.'

'Matriarch, Foxeye is still weak, Croptail is weaning and vulnerable to the wolves, Wolfnose can barely walk. The digging is exhausting all of us—'

The Matriarch's great jaw ceased its fore-and-back motion. 'You're right,' she said.

'. . . What?'

'We're in no fit state to have set off on an expedition like this. That's what you're leading up to, isn't it? But I wonder if you realise what peril we are in, little Silverhair. *Where water vanishes, sanity soon follows.* That's what the Cycle teaches. Thirst maddens us. Soon, without water, we would turn on each other . . . I have to avoid that at all costs, for we would be destroyed.

'Perhaps if we had stayed where we were, the thaw might have come to us before we all died of thirst. But that was not my judgement,' Owlheart growled. 'And that is the essence of being Matriarch, Silverhair. Sometimes there are no good choices: only a series of bad ones.'

'And so we are forced to risk all our lives on the bounty of a seep-hole,' Silverhair protested.

'*The art of travelling is to pick the least dangerous path.*' That was another line from the Cycle, a teaching of the great Matriarch, Ganesha the Wise.

Owlheart was turning away, evidently intent on resuming her interrupted feeding.

But still Silverhair wasn't done. She blurted: 'Maybe the old ways aren't the right ways any more.'

Owlheart snorted. 'Have you been talking to Lop-ear again?'

Silverhair was indignant. 'I don't need Lop-ear to tell me how to think.'

'The defiant one, aren't you? Tell me what has brought on this sudden doubt.'

And Silverhair spoke to the Matriarch again of the monster she had encountered on the ice floe. 'So you see, if there is such a strange creature in the world, who knows what else there is to find? *The world is changing.* Anyone can see that. It's why the winters are warmer, why the rich grass and shrubs are harder to find. But maybe there's some good for us in all this. If we only go searching – listen with open ears – we might discover—'

Owlheart cut her off with a slap of her trunk, hard enough to sting. 'Listen to me carefully. There is nothing for us in what you saw at the coast: nothing but misery and pain and death. Do you understand?'

'Won't you even tell me what it means?'

'We won't talk of this again, Silverhair,' said Owlheart, and she turned her massive back.

There was a commotion at Silverhair's feet. Gloomy, frustrated, she looked down. She saw a little animated bundle of orange hair, smelled the warm, cloying aroma of milk. It was Sunfire. The calf trotted over to the Matriarch's fresh dung, and began to poke into the warm, salty goodies with her trunk. Soon she was totally absorbed. Silverhair, watching fondly, wished she could be like that again, trotting after her own concerns, in a state of blissful, unmarked innocence.

Eggtusk came up. His giant, inward-curving tusks were looming over her, silhouetted against the sky. For a while he walked with her.

She saw that they had become isolated from the rest of the Family. And, with a flash of intuition, she saw why he had approached her. 'Eggtusk—'

'What?'

'The thing I saw on the ice floe, in the south. *You know what it is*, don't you?'

He regarded her. His words, coming deep from the hollow of his chest, were coupled with an unnatural stillness of his great head. It made her feel small and weak.

'Listen to me very carefully,' he said. 'Owlheart is right.

You must not go there again. And pray to Kilukpuk that your monster did not recognise you, that it does not track you here.'

'Why? It looked weaker than a wolf cub.'

'Perhaps it did,' said Eggtusk sadly. 'But that little beast was stronger than you, stronger than me – than all of us put together. It was the beast which the Cycle tells us can never be fought.'

'You mean—'

'*It was a Lost*, little one. It was a Lost, on our Island. *Now* do you see?' Eggtusk seemed to be trembling, and that struck a deep dread into Silverhair's heart, for she had never seen the great Eggtusk afraid of anything before—

Snagtooth screamed.

'Circle!' snapped the Matriarch.

Almost without thinking, Silverhair found herself joining the others in a tight circle around Snagtooth, with the calves cowering inside, and the adults arrayed on the outside, their tusks and trunks pointing outward, huge and intimidating, ready to beat off any predator or threat.

But Silverhair knew that there were no predators involved here – nobody, in fact, but Snagtooth herself.

Snagtooth raised her head from the scraped-out hole. Her right tusk was snapped off, almost at the root where it was embedded in her face. Instead of the smooth spiral of ivory she had carried before, there was now only a broken stump, its edge rimmed by jagged, bone-like fragments. A dark fluid dripped from the tusk's hollow core; it was pulp, the living flesh of the tusk. And the skin around the tusk was ripped and bleeding heavily.

Each of the mammoths felt the pain of the break as if it was their own. Sunfire, the infant, squealed in horror and burrowed under her mother's skirt of hair.

Eggtusk lowered his trunk and reached into the hole in the ground. With some effort, he pulled out the rest of the broken tusk. 'She trapped it under a boulder that was frozen in the ground,' he said. 'Simple as that. By Kilukpuk's hairy anus, what a terrible thing. You always were too impatient, Snagtooth—'

Snagtooth howled. With tears coursing down the hair on her face, she made to charge him, like a Bull on musth, with her one remaining tusk.

Eggtusk, startled, held his ground and, with a twist of his own mighty tusks, deflected her easily, without harming her.

Owlheart stepped between them angrily. 'Enough. Leave her be, Eggtusk.'

Eggtusk withdrew, growling.

Owlheart laid her trunk over Snagtooth's neck, and stroked her mouth and eyes. 'He was right, you know. Your teeth are brittle – why do you think you are called Snagtooth in the first place? – and a tusk is nothing but a giant tooth . . . The best thing to do is to freeze that stump, or otherwise the pulp will grow infected, and we will cake it with clay to stop the bleeding. You two,' she said to Lop-ear and Silverhair, 'get on with your digging. It's all the more important now.'

She led Snagtooth away from the others.

With Lop-ear, Silverhair resumed her work, trying to ignore the splashes of tusk pulp and splinters of ivory which disfigured the ground.

At last – after hacking at such cost through a trunk's-length of permafrost – they broke through to seep-water. But the water was low and brackish, so thin it took long heartbeats for Silverhair to suck up as much as a trunkful.

The hole was too deep for the infants' short trunks to reach the water, so Foxeye and Silverhair let water from their own trunks trickle into the mouths of the younger ones. Sunfire was still learning to drink; she spilled more water than she swallowed.

Wolfnose could not bend so easily, and she too had difficulty reaching the water. But she refused any help, proudly; she insisted she had drunk enough by her own efforts, and walked stiffly away.

The mammoths drank as much as the seep-hole would offer them. But it wasn't enough, and there was still no sign of the spring thaw.

'We have to go on,' said Owlheart solemnly. 'Further west, to the land beneath the glaciers. There, at this time of year, meltwater will be found running over the land. That's where we must go.'

That was a land unknown to Silverhair – and a dangerous place, for sometimes the meltwater would come from the glaciers in great deluges that could carve out a new landscape, stranding or trapping unwary wanderers. That the Matriarch was prepared to take such a risk was a measure of the seriousness of the situation; but nevertheless Silverhair felt a prick of interest that she would be going somewhere new.

They slept before moving on.

The short day was soon over. A hard Moon sailed into the sky, lighting up high clouds of ice. The silence of the Arctic night settled on the Family, a huge emptiness broken only by the mewling of Sunfire at her mother's breast, and Snagtooth's growled complaints at the pain of her shattered tusk.

Silverhair could feel the cold penetrate her guard hair and

underwool, through her flesh to her bones. Perhaps, she thought, this is how it will feel to grow old.

The Moon was still rising when Owlheart roused them and told them it was time to proceed.

Chapter Six

THE MOUNTAINS AT THE END OF THE WORLD

Cold, dry nights, lengthening days. Sometimes a dense grey fog would descend on the mammoths, wrapping them in obscurity. Nevertheless the full summer was approaching. Each night the sun dipped to the horizon, becoming lost in the mist, but the sky grew no darker than a rich blue, speckled with stars.

There came a night when the sun did not set. By day it rolled along the horizon, distorted by refraction and mist; but even at midnight slivers of ruddy light were visible, casting shadows that crossed the land from horizon to horizon, and the sky was filled with a wan glow that lacked warmth but was sufficient to banish the stars. Silverhair knew that the axis of the planet had reached that point in its annual round where it was tipped towards the sun, and there would be no true darkness for a hundred days.

The land, here in the Island's northern plain, rolled to the horizon with a sense of immensity. There was little snow or ice; the wind blew too strongly and steadily for that. And it was a *flat* place. The sparse plants that clung to life here – tough grasses resistant to both frost and drought, small shrubs like sagebrush, wormwood, even rhododendron – all grew low, with short branches and strong root systems to resist the scouring effects of the wind. Even the dwarf willows cowered against the ground, their branches sprawled over the rock, dug in.

When the wind picked up it moaned through the sparse grass with an eerie intensity.

At last the Mountains at the End of the World hove into Silverhair's view. In the low sunlight the upper slopes of the Mountains were bathed in a vibrant pink glow, which reflected down on to the slopes beneath where blue shadows pooled, the colours mixing to indigo and mauve.

As the land rose towards the Mountains, gathering like a great rocky wave, it became steadily more stony and barren. Here nothing grew save sickly coloured lichen, useless for the mammoths to eat.

And the land showed the battle-scars left by the huge warring forces of the past: giant scratches in the rock, boulders and shattered scree thrown as if at random over the landscape, smooth-sided gouges cut into what soil remained. It was, rumbled Wolfnose, the mark of the ancient ice sheets which had once lain a mile thick over this land.

They approached a dark wall of spruce trees, unexpected so far north. Silverhair wondered if some outcropping of the Earth's inner warmth was working here to sustain these trees. The Family were forced to push further north, to skirt the trees and the barren land that surrounded them.

The light changed. It became strange: almost greenish in its unnaturally pale tinge. Looking up, Silverhair saw ice clouds scudding hard across the sky. A flock of ptarmigan in brilliant white plumage took off like a snow flurry, and flew into the

Mountains. Their display calls echoed eerily from the rocky walls.

'Storm coming.'

She turned, and found the bulk of Eggtusk alongside her.

'And that's new,' he growled, indicating the neck of forest ahead of them. 'New since the last time the Family came this way.'

'When was that?'

'Before you were born. Every year the forest pushes further north, like pond scum on the great backside of Kilukpuk. Except that, unlike Kilukpuk, we can't scrape the land clean on a rock! Bah.'

Overhead, the greenish light was obscured by a layer of black, scudding clouds.

As the storm gathered they continued to skirt the forest, heading north-east, until they came to the fringe of the Mountains at the End of the World.

They walked past the eroded foothills of a mountain, which loomed above Silverhair. It was a severe black-brown cone, the glaciers were white ribbons wrapped around it. Yellow sunlight gleamed through the mountain's deep, ice-cut valleys.

High above her there was a snow avalanche: it poured down the mountain in a mighty, drawn-out whisper, and for a while she was enveloped in dancing flakes. And now the wind increased, coming through the towering rock pinnacles that rose above her, a keening lament that resonated in her skull. A whirr of ice splinters came scuttling across the rock shelf's surface; with every further step she took she crunched on crystals.

This was a noisy place. The cliff faces were alive with the crack of ice, the rustle and clatter of falling scree. Silverhair knew this was the voice of rock and ice, the frost's slow reworking of the upraised landscape.

Her spirit was lifted. The violence of the land exhilarated her.

Such was the clamour of ice and rock and wind from this huge barrier that even with their acute hearing, Silverhair's Family knew nothing of the land beyond the Mountains at the End of the World. Not even Longtusk himself had been able to glean the secrets of the lands which might lie to the north. Perhaps there was nothing beyond, nothing but mist and sky. But if this truly was the End of the World, Silverhair thought, then there could be no better marker than these Mountains.

Now they came to the snout of one of the great glaciers. The glacier was a river of ice, flowing with invisible slowness, its smooth curves tinted blue, surprisingly clean and beautiful.

The glacier had poured, creaking, down from the Mountains, carving and shattering the rock as it proceeded. But here, where it spilled on to the rocky plain, the pressure on that ice river was receding. The glacier calved into slices and towers, some of which had fallen to lie smashed in great blocks at her feet. Silverhair found herself walking amid sculptures of ice and snow, carved by the wind and rain into columns and wings and boulders, adorned with convoluted frills and laces, extraordinarily delicate and intricate.

But the land here was difficult. The mammoths were forced to thread their way between the ice blocks and the moraines: uneven mounds of sharp-edged debris, scoured by the glacier from the Mountains and deposited here. The wind was hard now, spilling off the Mountains. It plastered the mammoths' hair against their bodies, and Silverhair could feel it lashing against her eyes.

At last the glacier itself loomed above them, a wall of green ice and windswept snow.

Silverhair was stunned by the glacier's scale. The mammoths were the largest creatures in this landscape, and yet the ice wall before her was so tall its top was lost in mist that lingered above, as if reaching to the very clouds. Where the low sunlight caught the ice it shone a rich white-blue, as if stars were trapped within its structure; but loose fragments scattered over its surface sparkled like dew.

A pair of Arctic foxes sprinted past, probably a mating pair, their sleek white forms hard to see against the ice; Silverhair heard the foxes' complex calls to each other.

There was a flash, and thunder cracked; the mammoths flinched.

'Take it easy,' shouted Eggtusk, his trunk aloft, sniffing for danger. 'That was well to the south of us. Probably struck in that forest we skirted.'

Silverhair looked that way. There was another flash, and this time she saw the lightning bolt, liquid fire that shot down into the forest from the low clouds racing above. The bolt struck a tree, which fell into the forest with a crash. And a steady, reddish glow was gathering in the heart of the forest.

Fire.

Now the rain came, a hard, driving, almost horizontal sheet of water, laced with snow and hailstones.

The Matriarch had to shout and gesture. 'We'll climb up towards the Mountains. Maybe we can shelter until this passes. Silverhair, look after Foxeye and the calves. The rest of you help Wolfnose. Hurry now.'

The Family moved to obey.

. . . Save for Lop-ear, who came up to Silverhair. 'I'm worried about that fire,' he said. 'The grasses here are as dry as a bone, and with that wind, it could be on us in seconds.'

She looked towards the forest. The light of the fire did seem to be spreading. 'But it's a long way away,' she said. 'And the rain—'

'Is hard but it's just gusting. Not enough to extinguish the forest, or even soak the grass.'

Soft wet snow lashed around them.

Silverhair looked for the infant, Sunfire. Foxeye was anxiously tugging at the baby's ear. But the calf was half-lying on the frozen ground, mewling pitiably. The snow had soaked into her sparse, spiky fur, making it lie flat against her compact little body; Silverhair could see lumpy ribs and backbone protruding through a too-thin layer of fat and flesh.

She stood with Foxeye and, by pulling at Sunfire's ears and trunk, managed to cajole the calf to her feet. Then Silverhair and Foxeye stood one to either side of the infant, supporting her tiny bulk against them. Silverhair could feel the calf shiver against her own stolid legs.

They tried to move her forward, away from the spreading flames. But the bedraggled Sunfire was too exhausted to move.

Silverhair looked back over her shoulder, anxiously. Fanned by the swirling wind, the fire had taken a firm hold in the stand of trees behind them, and an ominous red light was spreading through the gaunt black trunks. Already she could see flames licking at the dry grass of the slice of exposed tundra that lay between the mammoths and the forest.

But her awareness of the fire spread far beyond the limited sense of sight. She could smell the gathering stink of wood succumbing to the flames, the sour stench of burning sap; hear the pop and hiss of the moist wood. She understood the fire, felt it on a deep level; it was as if a flame was burning through the world map she carried in her head.

She knew they had to flee. But she and Foxeye could not handle the calf on their own. She turned, looking for help.

Poor Wolfnose was turning away from the fire, slow and

stately as some giant hairy iceberg, but her stiff legs were unable to carry her as once they had. 'I'm not a calf any more, you know . . .' Owlheart, Eggtusk and Lop-ear were striving to help her. Their giant bulks were walls of soaked fur to either side of Wolfnose, and Lop-ear had settled himself behind her, and was pushing at her rear with his lowered forehead. Owlheart, helping with her mother and trumpeting instructions to the Family as a whole, was even finding time to wrap a reassuring trunk over the head of Croptail; the young Bull stuck close to the Matriarch.

But that left nobody to help Silverhair and Foxeye with the calf.

Nobody – except their aunt, Snagtooth, who stood away from the others, still mewling like a distressed calf over her shattered tusk.

Silverhair turned to Foxeye and raised her trunk. 'Wait here.'

Foxeye, exhausted herself, was close to panic. 'Silverhair – don't leave me—'

'I'll be back.' She trotted quickly over to Snagtooth.

The mud Owlheart had caked over the smashed tusk stump was beginning to streak over Snagtooth's fur and expose the mess of blood and pulp that lay beneath. Snagtooth's eyes were filled with a desolate misery, and Silverhair felt a stab of sympathy, for the wound did look agonising. But, for now, she knew she had to put that from her mind.

She grabbed her aunt's trunk and pulled. 'Come on. Foxeye needs your help.'

'I can't. You'll have to cope. I have to look after myself.' And Snagtooth snatched her trunk back.

Silverhair growled, reached up with her trunk and grabbed Snagtooth's healthy tusk. 'If there was anybody else I wouldn't care,' she rumbled. 'But there isn't anybody else.' She moved closer to Snagtooth and spoke again, loud enough to be audible over the howling of the storm, soft enough so nobody else could hear. 'Are you going to come with me, or are you going to make me drag you?'

For long heartbeats Snagtooth stared down at Silverhair. Snagtooth was older and, massive for a Cow, a good bit bigger than Silverhair. Now Silverhair wondered if Snagtooth would call her bluff and challenge her – and if she did, whether Silverhair could cope with her, despite the smashed tusk.

But Snagtooth backed down. 'Very well. But you aren't Matriarch yet, little Silverhair. I won't forget this.'

She turned away and, with evident reluctance, made her way towards Foxeye and the slumping Sunfire.

Silverhair felt chilled to the core, as if she'd taken a bellyful of snow.

It was slow going. The two groups of Family, huddled around the calf and the proud old Cow, seemed to crawl across the hard ground.

Here and there the snow was drifting into deceptively deep pockets. Mammoths always have difficulty traversing deep snow: now Silverhair felt her legs sink into the soft, slushy whiteness, and it pushed like a rising tide up around the long hair of her belly, chilling her dugs. In the deepest of the drifts she had to work hard, with Foxeye, to keep the calf's head and trunk above the level of the snow.

And all the time Silverhair could sense the fire pooling over the dry ground. The snow was having no effect now, such was the heat the fire was generating, and she knew their only chance was to outrun it. She stayed close to Sunfire, sheltering the calf from the wind and encouraging her to hurry – and she tried to contain her own rising panic.

But now they were brought to a halt.

Silverhair found herself on the bank of a stream that bubbled its way from the base of the ice and across the rocky land. She could see where the stream was already cutting into the loose soil and debris scattered over the rock, and depositing small stones from within the glacier. The mammoths' deep knowledge of their Island could not have helped them predict they would encounter this barrier, for every year the runoff streams reshaped the landscape. And the stream was wide, clearly too deep to ford or even to swim.

The mammoths stood clustered together against the wind, staring at the rushing water with dismay. Silverhair, blocked, felt baffled, frustrated, and filled with a deep dread that reached back to her near-drowning as a calf. It was a bitter irony, for a runoff stream like this was exactly what they had come looking for: and now it lay in their way.

She found Lop-ear standing with her. 'We're in trouble,' he said. 'Look around, Silverhair. The runoff here. The forest over there, where the fire is coming from. Behind us, the Mountains . . .'

Suddenly she understood.

They had got themselves trapped here, by river and Mountains and forest, as surely as if they had all plunged into a kettle hole.

Now Eggtusk came to them. 'We can't cross the stream,' he said bluntly.

'But—' said Lop-ear.

Eggtusk ignored him. 'It's not a time for debate. We have to move on. We can't go north; that way will soon take us into the Mountains. So we follow the stream south. The stream will get broad and shallow and maybe there'll be somewhere to cross. That's what Owlheart has ordered, and I agree with her.'

He turned away, preparing to go back to Wolfnose, but Lop-ear touched his trunk. 'Eggtusk, wait. Going south won't work. The fire will reach us before we—'

Eggtusk quoted the Cycle. '*The Matriarch has given her orders, and we follow.*'

Lop-ear cried, 'Not to our deaths!'

In the middle of the storm, there was a moment of shocked stillness.

Silverhair, startled, could not remember anyone continuing to argue with Eggtusk after such a warning.

Nor, evidently, could Eggtusk.

Eggtusk lifted his great head high over Lop-ear; he was an imposing mass of muscle, flesh and wiry, mud-brown hair. 'Any more talk like that and I'll silence you for good. You'll frighten the calves.'

'They should be frightened!'

Hastily Silverhair shoved her trunk into Lop-ear's pink, warm mouth to silence him. 'Come on,' she said. Pulling him with her trunk, nudging him with her flank, she led him away from a glaring Eggtusk.

But she felt a deep chill. Lop-ear, with his fast, unusual mind, could sometimes be distracted, a little strange. But she had never seen him so agitated.

. . . And what, she thought with a deep shiver, if he is right? He's been right about so many things in the past. What if we really are just walking to our deaths?

Still Lop-ear called. But the wind snatched away his words, and nobody listened.

Chapter Seven

THE BARRIER

With Foxeye and a reluctant Snagtooth, Silverhair shepherded a trembling, unsteady Sunfire along the bank of the runoff stream.

Although the depth and ferocity of the central channel gradually reduced, the stream spread further over the surrounding ground, and sheets of water ran over the rock. The cloudy water made the rock slick enough to cause even the tough sole of a mammoth's foot to slip, and several times poor Sunfire had to be rescued from stumbles.

Meanwhile the storm mounted in ferocity, with gigantic clatters from the sky and startling bolts of lightning and a wind that swirled unpredictably, slamming heavy wet snowflakes into Silverhair's face.

And all the time she could sense the fire as it spread through the dry old grass towards them.

Lop-ear was helping Owlheart and Eggtusk with Wolfnose's cautious progress. But he was still calling to the sky, complaining and prophesying doom. Right now the Matriarch and the old Bull were too busy to deal with him, but Silverhair knew he would pay for his ill-discipline later.

She came to a young spruce, lying across the rocky ground near the stream. It neatly blocked the mammoths' path.

The little group broke up again. Foxeye, panting and near exhaustion, tucked her infant under her belly-hair curtain. Snagtooth, yowling complaints about her tusk, turned away from the others and scrabbled in the cold mud of the stream bank to cover her wound once more.

Silverhair stepped forward. She saw that the tree's roots had sunk themselves into a shallow soil that was now overrun by the stream; when the soil was washed away, the tree had fallen. The tree itself would not be difficult to cross. They could all climb over, probably, or with a little effort they could even push it out of the way.

But the tree was only an outlier of the spruce forest. Other trees grew here, small and stunted and sparsely separated – and some of them, too, had been felled by the runoff – and she could see that a little further south the trees grew more densely, and she could smell the thick, damp mulch of the forest floor.

Eggtusk, with Owlheart, came up to her. Eggtusk saw the fallen tree. 'By Kilukpuk's gravel-stuffed navel. That's all we need.'

'We'll have to climb over it,' said Owlheart.

'Yes. If we get Wolfnose over first—'

But suddenly Lop-ear was here, standing head to head with Eggtusk. He was bedraggled, muttering, excited, eyes wide and full of reflected lightning. 'No. Don't you see? This is the answer. If we push this fallen tree over *there* – and then go further towards the forest to find more—'

In the flickering light of the storm, the old Bull stood as solid as if he had grown out of the rock. Owlheart and Wolfnose watched, their icy disapproval of Lop-ear's youthful antics obvious.

Eggtusk said, 'You're risking all our lives by wasting time like this.'

Silverhair hurried forward. 'What are you trying to say, Lop-ear?'

'I can't tell you!' he cried. 'I just *know*, if we push the trees together, and—'

'He's going rogue,' said Owlheart now. The Matriarch lumbered forward, and glowered down at the prancing Lop-ear. 'I always knew this calf would be trouble. All his talk of *chang-ing* things. He's more like one of the Lost than a mammoth.'

'Listen to me!' Lop-ear was trumpeting now. He ran to Owlheart, who was turning away, and grabbed at her trunk. 'Listen to me—'

Now Eggtusk's massive bulk was between them. 'You don't touch the Matriarch like that.'

'But you must *listen*.'

'Perhaps you'll listen to this,' roared Eggtusk, and he tusked the ground.

It was a challenge.

Eggtusk and Lop-ear faced each other, trunks lowered, ears flaring, gazes locked. Lop-ear was trembling, and Eggtusk seemed to tower over him, his great incurving tusks poised over his head.

Bull mammoths have their own society, a society of bachelor herds independent of the Families of Cows and calves controlled by the Matriarchs. It is a warrior society, based on continual tests of strength and dominance. Normally, unless enraged by musth, a young Bull like Lop-ear would never challenge a giant tusker like Eggtusk – or if challenged, he would soon back down.

Now Silverhair waited for Lop-ear to stretch his trunk at Eggtusk to show his deference.

But Lop-ear made no such sign.

Silverhair rushed forward. 'Eggtusk, please. He didn't mean—'

But Owlheart was in her way, solid as a boulder. 'Stay back, child. This is a matter for the Bulls.'

Lop-ear raised his head and made the first blow, dashing his tusks against Eggtusk's. There was a knock of ivory on ivory, as if one great tree was being smashed into another.

The older Bull did not so much as flinch.

Again Lop-ear stabbed at Eggtusk's face. But this time Eggtusk dipped sideways, so that Lop-ear's thrust missed. Eggtusk brought his massive head down and slammed his forehead against Lop-ear's temple.

Lop-ear cried out, and stumbled back.

Eggtusk trumpeted and lumbered forward. Lop-ear turned to face him, both mammoths trying to stay head-on; if either was turned his opponent could easily knock him down or even stab him.

Still the rain howled around them, still the lightning split the sky, and still the gathering light and smoke-stink of the fire filled Silverhair's head. She was peripherally aware of the other mammoths: Foxeye's weary disbelief, Snagtooth's disdain, Croptail's childish excitement.

'I don't want to fight you,' said Lop-ear. He was panting hard, and blood was seeping from a wound in his temple. 'But if that's what I have to do to make you listen—'

Wordlessly Eggtusk trumpeted once more and raised his massive tusks. The sleetish rain swirled around them, and water dripped from the tusks' cruel tips.

Lop-ear lunged. But once again Eggtusk side-stepped, and he brought his own tusks crashing down on Lop-ear's domed head with a splintering crash.

Silverhair, horrified, trumpeted in alarm.

The younger Bull bellowed, and fell to his knees.

Eggtusk turned again, and his tusks slashed at Lop-ear's foreleg, cutting through fur and flesh and drawing thick blood.

For a heartbeat, two, Lop-ear did not move. His face was wreathed in steam, and his great form shuddered.

But then, once more, he clambered stiffly to his feet and turned to face Eggtusk again.

Fights between unmatched Bulls are usually resolved quickly, Silverhair knew. Usually, it would be enough for Eggtusk to raise his great tusks for a junior like Lop-ear to back away.

Usually. But this was not a normal fight.

Silverhair tugged at Owlheart's trunk. 'Matriarch, you have to stop this.'

Owlheart quoted the Cycle. '*To fight is the way of the Bull—*'

'This isn't about dominance,' Silverhair said. 'Don't you see?'

But once again Lop-ear was facing Eggtusk. The space between their staring eyes was filled with tangled hair and steaming breath.

With blood smeared over the dome of his head, Lop-ear charged again.

The Bulls met once more, in a splintering crunch of ivory. Silverhair saw that their curving tusks were locked together. This was a risky tactic for both the combatants, for the tusks could become locked inextricably, taking both mammoths to their deaths.

The Bulls wrestled. Lop-ear bellowed, resisting Eggtusk.

But the older Bull was much stronger. With a smooth, steady, irresistible effort, Eggtusk twisted his head to one side. Lop-ear pawed at the ground, but it was slick and muddy, and the pads of his feet slipped.

It was over in heartbeats.

His tusks still locked to Eggtusk's, Lop-ear crashed to the ground.

Eggtusk stood over the helpless younger Bull, his eyes hard. Silverhair saw that he might twist further, surely snapping Lop-ear's neck – or he might withdraw his tusks and stab down sharply, driving his ivory into Lop-ear's helpless carcass.

The storm cracked over their heads, and for an instant the lightning picked out the silhouette of Eggtusk's giant deformed tusk.

Eggtusk braced himself for the final thrust.

'*No.*'

The commanding rumble made Eggtusk hesitate.

The voice had been Wolfnose's. The old Cow, once the Matriarch, was coming forward. The rain dripped unheeded from her tangled hair, and only a smear of tears around her deep old eyes betrayed the pain of her legs.

Eggtusk said, 'Wolfnose . . .?'

'Let him up, Eggtusk.'

In the silence that followed, Silverhair could see that they were all waiting for the Matriarch's response. It was wrong for a Cow to interfere in the affairs of Bulls. And it was wrong for any Cow – even a former Matriarch, like Wolfnose – to usurp the authority of the Matriarch herself.

But Owlheart was keeping her counsel.

Eggtusk growled. Then he lowered his head, dropped his trunk, and allowed Lop-ear to clamber to his feet.

The younger Bull stood shakily, his hair matted with mud.

He was bleeding heavily from the wounds to his leg and temple.

'This must stop,' said Wolfnose.

Eggtusk stiffened. 'But the Cycle—'

'I know the Cycle as well as any of you,' said Wolfnose. Her voice was even, yet powerful enough to be heard over the bellow of the storm. Once, Silverhair thought, this must have been a formidable Matriarch indeed. 'But,' Wolfnose went on, 'Ganesha taught us there are times when the Cycle can't help us. Look at us: lost, bedraggled, trapped . . . You will win your fight, Eggtusk. But what value is it? For we shall soon die, trapped here between forest and fire – all of us, even the infant. And then what?' She turned her great head and glared at them, one by one. 'When was the last time you saw another Family? And you? When was the last time you heard a contact rumble, at morning or evening? *What if we are alone – the last Family of all?* It's possible, isn't it? I tell you, if it's true, and if we do die here, then it all dies with us – after more generations than there are stars in the winter sky.'

And Silverhair, standing in the freezing rain, saw the truth, with sudden, devastating clarity. They had become a rabble, a few shivering, half-starved mammoths, a pathetic remnant of the great Clans which had once roamed here. A rabble so blinded by their own past and mythology they could not even act.

She stepped forward. 'Tell us what to do, Wolfnose.'

The old Cow stepped forward and laid her trunk over Lop-ear's splintered tusk. 'We must do what this bright young Bull says.'

Lop-ear – breathing hard, shivering, bloody – hesitated, as if waiting to be attacked once more. Then he turned to the runoff stream. 'The fallen tree-trunk,' he said, his voice blurred by blood and pain. 'Help me.' And he bent to the fallen tree, dug his tusks under it, and began to push it towards the stream. But it was much too heavy for him, exhausted as he was.

Wolfnose lumbered forward. With only a grimace to betray her pain, she forced her fused knees to bend, and she put her tusks alongside Lop-ear's and pushed with him.

The tree-trunk rocked, then fell back.

Silverhair ran forward. She squeezed between Wolfnose and Lop-ear, and rammed her head against the stubborn tree-trunk. With more hesitation, Eggtusk, Owlheart, and even Snagtooth joined in. Only Foxeye stayed back, shielding the calves.

Under the combined pressure of six adult mammoths, the tree-trunk soon popped out of its muddy groove in the ground, and rolled forward.

With a crunch of branches, the tree crashed over a boulder, and came to rest in the stream. It was so long it straddled almost the whole width of the stream. The water, bubbling, flowed over the tree and through its smashed branches.

The mammoths stood for a heartbeat, studying their work.

Silverhair looked back at Wolfnose. But Wolfnose was obviously drained; she stood with her trunk dangling, eyes closed, rain sleeting off her back.

Silverhair turned to Lop-ear. 'It's your idea, Lop-ear. Tell us what to do next.'

Now that he was being taken seriously, Lop-ear looked even more nervous and agitated than before. 'More trees! That's it. Pile them on this one. Any you can find. And anything else – boulders, shrubs—'

Eggtusk growled. 'By the lemmings that burrow in the stinking armpits of Kilukpuk: what madness is this?'

Owlheart said dryly, 'We may as well see it through, Eggtusk. Come on.' And she lumbered further up the stream, to a tumbled sapling.

With the Matriarch's implicit approval, the others hurried to work.

Silverhair helped Eggtusk haul another huge tree up the stream. But most of the fallen trees were simply too massive to move.

Lop-ear led them to a small stand of saplings, most of them still upright, and began to barge the smallest of them with his head. 'These will do,' he said. 'Smash them off and take them to the stream.'

Silverhair joined in. This, at least, was familiar. Mammoths will often break and push over young trees; the apparently destructive act serves to clear the land and maintain its openness, and thus the health of the tundra.

So the barrier grew, higgledy-piggledy, with branches and stones and even whole bushes, their roots still dripping with dirt, being thrown on it. Even little Croptail helped, rolling boulders into the stream, where they clattered to rest against the growing pile of debris.

As the barrier grew, the water of the runoff was evidently having trouble penetrating the thickening mass of foliage, rocks and dirt. At last, it began to form a brimming pool behind the pile.

And, ahead of it, the stream's volume was greatly reduced, to a sluggish brook that crawled through the muddy channel. Silverhair stared in amazement, suddenly understanding what Lop-ear had intended.

Lop-ear stood on the bank of the stream. His head was smeared with blood and mud, and his belly hairs, soaked through, were beginning to stiffen with frost. But when he looked on his work he raised his trunk and trumpeted with triumph. 'That's it! *We can cross now.*'

'By Kilukpuk's fetid breath,' growled Eggtusk. 'It's muddy, and boggy – it won't be easy – but, yes, we should be able to ford there now. I never expected to say this, Lop-ear, but there may be something useful about you after all.'

'We should move fast,' said Lop-ear, apparently indifferent to Eggtusk's praise. 'The water is still rising. When it reaches the top of the barrier it will come rushing over, just as hard as before.'

'And besides,' Silverhair pointed out, 'that fire hasn't stopped burning.'

The Matriarch, who had already taken in the situation, brayed a sharp command, and the mammoths prepared for the crossing.

They got the calves across first.

Croptail had no difficulty. He slid down the muddy bank into the water, then emerged to shake himself dry and scramble up the far side to his mother's waiting trunk. Silverhair heard him squeal in delight, as if it was all a game.

Eggtusk was the key to getting Sunfire across. The great Bull plunged willingly into the river, sinking into freezing mud and water that lapped over his belly. The calf slithered down into the ditch and clambered across Eggtusk's broad, patient back.

Then, with Sunfire safely across, Lop-ear reached down and thrust forward a foot for Eggtusk to grasp with his trunk. Eggtusk pulled himself out, huffing mightily, with Lop-ear scrambling to hold his position, and Owlheart and Silverhair threw bark and twigs beneath Eggtusk's feet to help him climb.

Wolfnose was more difficult.

Owlheart tugged gently at her mother's trunk. 'Come now.'

Wolfnose opened her eyes within their nests of wrinkles, regarded her daughter, and with a sigh lifted her feet from the clinging, icy mud. The others gathered around her, Eggtusk behind her. But when she came to the slippery bank of the stream, Wolfnose stopped.

'I am weary,' said Wolfnose slowly. 'Leave me. I will sleep first.'

Owlheart stood before her, helpless; and Silverhair felt her heart sink.

But Eggtusk growled, and he began to butt Wolfnose's backside, quite disrespectfully. 'I – have – had – enough – of *this*!'

Almost against her will, Wolfnose was soon hobbling down the slippery bank. Silverhair and the others quickly gathered around her, helping her to stay on her feet. Wolfnose splashed, hard, into the cold, turbulent stream that emerged from beneath Lop-ear's impromptu dam. Once there, breathing heavily, she found it hard to scramble out. But Eggtusk plunged belly-deep into the clinging mud and shoved gamely at the old Cow's rear.

At last, with much scrambling, pushing and pulling, they had Wolfnose safely lodged on the far bank.

Not long after they had crossed, the water came brimming over the barrier, like a trunk emptying into a great mouth. The barrier fell apart, the trees scattering down the renewed stream like twigs, and it was as if the place they had forded had never been.

The storm blew itself out.

Silverhair watched as the fire came billowing across the tundra, at last reaching the bank they had left behind. But as the rain grew more liquid – and as the dry grass was consumed, with rain hissing over the scorched ground – the fire died.

Silverhair and Lop-ear emerged from the forest, and stood on the rocky ground overlooking the stream. On the far side of the stream the ground was blackened and steaming, with here and there the burned-out stump of a sapling spruce protruding from the ground.

A spectacular sheet of golden light, from broken clouds at the horizon, shimmered beneath the remaining grey clouds above.

'We'll have to move on soon,' said Lop-ear. 'There isn't anything for us to eat on this stony ground . . .'

'The fire would have killed us,' said Silverhair. She was certain she was right. Without Lop-ear's strange ingenuity, they would have perished. She looked down at the tree-trunks scattered along the length of the runoff stream. 'I don't know how you got the idea. But you saved us.'

'Yes,' Lop-ear said gloomily. 'But maybe Owlheart was right.'

'What do you mean?'

'I defied the Cycle. I defied Owlheart. I don't want that, Silverhair. I don't want to be different.'

'Lop-ear—'

'Maybe there *is* something of the Lost about me. Something dark.'

And with that, his eyes deep and troubled, he turned away.

No, thought Silverhair. No, you're wrong. Wolfnose, old and weary as she is, was able to see the value of new thinking – as was Ganesha the Wise before her.

The Cycle might not be able to guide them through the troubled times to come. It would require minds like Lop-ear's – new thinking, new solutions – if they were to survive.

She thought of the creature she had seen on the ice floe. One of the Lost, Eggtusk had said.

Her brain seethed with speculation over dangers and opportunities. Somehow, she knew, her destiny was bound up with the ugly, predatory monster she had encountered on that ice floe.

Destiny – or opportunity?

Silverhair surveyed the wreckage of the barrier a little longer. She tried to remember how it had been, what they had done to defeat the river. But already, she could not picture it.

And the runoff stream was dwindling. The glacier ice had been melted by the heat absorbed by the rock faces during the day. But as the sun sank, the rock cooled and the runoff slowed, reducing the torrents and gushes to mere trickles – which would, Silverhair realised ruefully, have been easy to cross.

She turned away and rejoined the others.

TWO

LOST

THE STORY OF THE CALVES OF KILUKPUK

Now (Silverhair said to Icebones) every mammoth has heard of the mother of us all: Kilukpuk, the Matriarch of Matriarchs, who grew up in a burrow in the time of the Reptiles. The tale I am going to tell you is of the end of Kilukpuk's life: two thousand Great-Years ago, when the Reptiles were long gone, and the world was young and warm and empty.

Now by this time Kilukpuk had been alive for a very long time.

Though she was the mother of us all, Kilukpuk was not like us. By now she more resembled the seals of the coast, with stubby legs and a nub of trunk. She had become so huge, in fact, that her body had sunk into the ground, turning it into a Swamp within which she dwelled.

But she had a womb as fertile as the sea.

One year she bore three calves.

The first was called Probos; the second was called Siros; the third was called Hyros.

There was no eldest or youngest, for they had all been born

at the same mighty instant. They all looked exactly the same. They played together happily, without envy or malice.

They were all equal.

And yet they were not.

Only one of them could be Matriarch, when Kilukpuk died.

As time wore on, the calves ceased to play with each other. They took to watching each other with suspicion and hostility, hoping to find some flaw or small crime they could report to their mother. At least, that is how Hyros and Siros behaved. For her part, Probos bore no ill-will to her sisters.

Kilukpuk floated in her Swamp, and showed no favour to any of her daughters.

Now Kilukpuk did not intend that her daughters should stay for ever in the Swamp, as she did. So, from the beginning, she had pushed her three daughters on to the land.

They had mewled and complained, wishing only to return to the comforting mud of the Swamp, and to snuggle once more against Kilukpuk's mighty dugs – which as you know were as big as the Mountains at the End of the World. But gradually the calves learned to browse at the grasses and nibble at the leaves of the trees, and ceased to miss the warm bath of the Swamp.

Now Hyros became very fond of the foliage of the lush trees of those days, and she became jealous if her sisters tried to share that particular bounty. It got to the point where Hyros started climbing trees to ensure she reached the juiciest leaves before her sisters, and she would leap from branch to branch and even between the trees to keep her sisters away, and she made a great crashing noise when she did so.

And Siros likewise became very fond of the fruits of the seas and rivers, and she became jealous if her sisters tried to share that particular bounty. It got to the point where Siros started swimming in the rivers and seas to ensure she reached the thickest reeds before her sisters, and she made a great galumphing, splashing noise while she did so.

Now, none of this troubled Probos. She knew that the grasses and sedges and herbs and bushes of the world were more than enough to feed her for the rest of her long life, and as many calves as she could imagine bearing. She tried to tell her sisters this: that they had nothing to fear from her or each other, for the world was rich enough to support all of them.

This enraged her sisters, for they thought Probos must be trying to trick them. And so, silently, separately, they hatched their plans against her.

One day, when Probos was browsing calmly on a lush patch of grass, she heard Hyros calling from a treetop: 'Oh, Probos!' She was so high up her voice sounded like a bird's cry. 'I want to show you how fond I am of you, sister. Here – I want you to have the very best and sweetest and fattest leaves I can find.' And Hyros began to hurl down great mouthfuls of bark and leaves and twigs, from the very tops of the trees.

Now Probos was a little bewildered. For the truth was, she had grown to relish the thin, aromatic flavour of the herbs and grasses. She found tree leaves thick and cloying and damp in her mouth, and the bark and twigs scratched at her lips and tongue. But she did not wish to offend her sister, and so she patiently began to eat the tree stuff.

For a day and a night Hyros fed her sister like this, unrelenting, and soon Probos's dung grew slippery with undigested masses of leaf. But still she would not offend her sister, and she patiently worked her way through the great piles on the ground.

Suddenly Hyros stopped throwing down the leaves. She thrust her small, mean face out of the foliage, and glared down at Probos, laughing. 'Look at you now! You will never be able to climb up here and steal my leaves!'

And when Probos looked down at herself, she found she had eaten so much she had grown huge – much bigger than her sisters, though not so big as Kilukpuk – so big that she could, surely, never again climb a tree. She looked up at Hyros sadly. 'Why have you tricked me, sister? I had no wish to share your leaves.'

But Hyros wasn't listening. She bounded off through her branches, laughing at what she had done.

Kilukpuk saw this, but said nothing.

A little while later, when Probos was grazing contentedly on a patch of particularly savoury herbs, she heard Siros calling from the river. 'Oh, Probos!' Siros barely poked her nose out of the water, and her voice sounded like the bubbling of a fish. 'I want to show you how fond I am of you, sister. Here – I want you to enjoy the sweetest water of all, with me. Come. Give me your nose.'

Now Probos was a little bewildered. For the truth was, she was quite happy with the water she lapped from small streams and puddles; she found river water cold and silty and full of weeds. But she patiently kneeled down and lowered her nose to her sister in the water.

Siros immediately clamped her teeth on the end of Probos's nose and began to pull. Through a clenched jaw she said, 'Now, you stand firm, sister; this will not take long.'

For a day and a night Siros dragged at her sister's nose like this, unrelenting, and soon Probos's nose was starting to stretch, longer and longer, like growing grass. And it hurt a great deal, as you can imagine! And while this was going on, she could not eat or drink, and her dung grew thin and watery and foul-smelling. But still she would not offend her sister, and patiently she let Siros wrench at her aching nose.

Suddenly Siros stopped pulling at Probos's nose. She opened

her jaws and slid back into the water, and Probos fell backwards.

Siros thrust her small, mean face out of the water, and glared up at Probos, laughing. 'Look at you now! What a ridiculous nose. With that in the way, you will never be able to slide through the water and steal my reeds!'

And when Probos looked down at herself, she found her nose had grown so long it dangled between her legs, all the way to the ground.

She looked down at Siros sadly. 'Why have you tricked me, sister? I didn't want to share your reeds or your water.'

But Siros wasn't listening. She turned and wriggled away through the water, laughing at what she had done.

Kilukpuk saw this, but said nothing.

The years passed, and at last the day came when Kilukpuk called her calves to her.

But the calves had changed.

Siros had now spent so long in the river and the sea that her skin had grown smooth, the hair flowing on it like water. And Hyros had spent so long in the trees that she had become small and agile, fast-moving and nervous.

As for Probos, she had a body like a boulder, and legs like mighty trees, and a nose she had learned to use as a trunk. And where Siros wriggled and flopped and Hyros skittered to and fro, Probos moved over the land as stately as the shadow of a cloud.

Kilukpuk hauled herself out of her Swamp. 'My teeth grow soft,' she said, 'and soon I will not be here to be your Matriarch. I know that the question of which of you shall follow me as Matriarch has much vexed you – some of you, at least. Here is what I have decided.'

And Hyros and Siros said together, 'Which of us? Oh, tell us. Which of us?'

Probos said nothing, but merely wept tears of Swamp water for her mother.

Kilukpuk said, 'You will all be Matriarch. And none of you will be Matriarch.'

Hyros and Siros fell silent, puzzled.

Kilukpuk said, 'You, Siros, are the Matriarch of the water. But the water is not yours. Even close to the land there will be many who will compete with you for fish and weeds and will hunt you down. But it is what you have stolen from your sisters, and it is what you wanted, and it is what you will have. Go now.'

And Siros squirmed around and flopped her way back to the water.

Now Kilukpuk said, 'You, Hyros, are the Matriarch of the trees. But the trees are not yours. You have made yourself small and weak and frightened, and that is how you will remain. Animals and birds will compete with you for leaves and bark and plants and will hunt you down. But it is what you have stolen from your sisters, and it is what you wanted, and it is what you will have. Go now.'

And Hyros clambered nervously to the branches of the tall trees.

That left only Probos, who waited patiently for her mother to speak. But Kilukpuk was weakening now, and her great body sank deeper into the water of the Swamp. She spat out fragments of tooth (so huge, by the way, they became glaciers where they fell). And she said to Probos, 'You stole nothing from your sisters. And yet what they stole from you has made you strong.

'Go, Probos. For the Earth is yours.

'With your great bulk you need fear no predator. With your strong and agile trunk you will become the cleverest animal in the world. Go now, Probos, Matriarch of the mammoths and all their Cousins who live on the land.'

Probos was greatly saddened; but she was a good calf who obeyed her Matriarch.

(And what Kilukpuk prophesied would come to pass, for each of Probos's calves and their calves to come. But that was for the future.)

Kilukpuk raised herself from the Swamp and called to her calves one last time. She said, 'You will rarely meet again; nor will your calves, or your calves' calves. But you will be Cousins for ever. You must not fight or kill each other. If you meet your Cousins you will assist each other, without question or hesitation or limit. You will make your calves swear this binding oath.'

Well, that was the end of the jealousy between the sisters. Hyros and Siros were remorseful, Probos was gladdened, and the three of them swore to hold true to Kilukpuk's command.

And that is why, as soon as she is old enough to speak, every calf is taught the Oath of Kilukpuk.

But as Kilukpuk sank back into her Swamp and prepared for her journey back into the Earth, she was saddened. For she knew she had not told even Probos, the best of her calves, the whole truth.

For, one day, there would be something for them *all* to fear – even mighty Probos.

Chapter One

THE PLAIN OF BONES

Arctic summer: the sun arced around the sky's north pole, somehow aimlessly, and at midnight it rolled lazily along the horizon. It was a single day, long and crystalline, that would last for two months, an endless day of feeding and breeding and dying.

At midnight Silverhair, walking slowly with her Family across the thawing plain, saw that she cast a shadow, ice-sharp, that stretched to the horizon. She felt oddly weighed down by the shadow, as if it were some immense tail she must drag around with her. But the light turned everything to gold, and made the bedraggled mammoths, with their clouds of loose moulting fur, glow as if on fire.

They reached an area of tundra new to Silverhair. The mammoths, exhausted by their adventures, spread slowly over the landscape. As the thaw arrived, they found enough to drink in the meltpools that gathered over the permafrost. On days that were excessively hot – because mammoths do not sweat – they would reduce heat by panting, or they would find patches of soft snow to stand in, sometimes eating mouthfuls of it.

The changes in the land were dramatic now; for, after a month of continuous daylight, the sun was high and hot enough to melt ice. Rock began to protrude through the thawing hillsides, and blue meltwater glimmered on the frozen lakes. As snow banks melted, drips became trickles, and gullies became streams, and rivers, marshes and ponds reformed. In sheltered valleys there were already patches of sedge and grass, green and meadow-like. After months of frozen whiteness the land was becoming an intricate pattern of black and white. This emerging panorama – shimmering with moist light, draped in mist and fog – was still wreathed in silence. But already the haunting calls of Arctic loons echoed to the sky from the meltpools.

The mammoths slept and fed in comparative comfort, and time wore away, slowly and unmarked.

Croptail tried to play with his sister, Sunfire, and his antics pleased the slower-moving adults, who would reach down trunk or tusk to allow the Bull calf to wrestle. But despite her mother's attention Sunfire was feeding badly and did not seem to be putting on weight, and her coat remained shabby and tangled. She spent most of her time tucked under her mother's belly hair, with her face clamped to one dug or other, while Foxeye whispered verses from the Cycle.

Still, it was, all things considered, a happy time. But Silverhair's spirits did not rise. She took to keeping her distance from the others – even from Lop-ear. She sought out patches of higher ground, her trunk raised.

For there was something carried to her by the wind off the sea – something that troubled her to the depths of her soul.

Wolfnose joined her. The old Cow stood alongside Silverhair, feeling with her trunk for rich patches of grass, then trapping tufts between her trunk and tusks and pulling them out.

Silverhair waited patiently. Wolfnose seemed to be moving more slowly than ever, and her rheumy eyes, constantly watering, must be almost blind now. So worn were Wolfnose's teeth it took her a long time to consume her daily meals. And when she passed dung, Silverhair saw that it was thin and sour-smelling, and contained much unchewed grass and twigs, and even some indigestible soil which Wolfnose, in her gathering blindness, had scooped into her mouth.

But, even as her body failed, Wolfnose seemed to be settling into a new contentment.

'This is a good time of year,' Wolfnose rumbled at last. She quoted the Cycle, '*When the day becomes endless, we shed our cares with our winter coats.*' She ground her grass contentedly, her great jaw moving back and forth. 'But you are not happy, child. Even my old eyes can see that much. What troubles you? Is it Sunfire?'

'I know Foxeye is looking after her well.'

'Sunfire was born in a difficult spring, a little too early. Now that summer is approaching, she will flourish like the tundra flowers—'

Silverhair blurted, 'Wolfnose – what do you *smell* here?'

For answer, Wolfnose patiently finished her mouthful of grass. Then she raised her trunk and turned it this way and that.

She said at last, 'There is the salt of the sea, to the west. There is the crisp fur of wolves, the sour droppings of lemmings, the stink of the guano of the gulls at the rocky coast . . .'

'But no mammoths.' Silverhair meant the complex of smells which characterised mammoths to each other: the smells of moist hair, dung, mother's milk.

Wolfnose said, 'No. But there is—'

Silverhair trembled. '*There is the stink of death – of dead mammoths.*'

Wolfnose lowered her trunk and turned calmly to Silverhair. 'It isn't what you think.'

Silverhair snapped. 'I'll tell you what I *do* think. I think that what I can smell is the stench of some other Family's rotting corpses.' She felt an unreasonable anger at Wolfnose's calm patience.

'I'll tell you the truth,' Wolfnose said. 'I can't say what's become of the other Families. It's certainly a long time – too long – since any of us met a mammoth from another Family, and you know my fears about *that*. But the scent you detect has another meaning. Something wonderful.'

'Wonderful? Can death be wonderful?'

'Yes. Come on.'

And with that, ripping another mouthful of grass from the clumps at her feet, Wolfnose began to walk towards the west.

Silverhair, startled, came to herself and hurried to catch up with Wolfnose. It did not take long, for Wolfnose's arthritic gait was so forced and slow that Silverhair thought even a glacier could outrun her now.

She called, 'Where are we going?'

'You'll find out when we arrive.'

The thawing ground was moist and fragile under Silverhair's feet, and every footstep left a scar. In fact the plain was criss-crossed by the trails of mammoths, wolves, foxes and other animals, left from last summer and the years before. It could take ten years for the fragile tundra to grow over a single footstep.

Overhead the snow geese were winging to their breeding grounds to the north, skein after skein of them passing across the blue sky. Occasionally, over the lakes, the geese plummeted from the sky to reach water through thin ice.

The tundra was wet, almost boggy, peppered by rivers, lakes, pools and peaty hummocks. Although there was so little rain it was actually a desert, the tundra was one of the most waterlogged lands on the planet. There was little evaporation into the cold air and virtually no absorption into the soil; for, just a short trunk's reach down through the carpet of plants, the ground was always frozen. This was the permafrost: nearly a mile deep, a layer of frozen soil that had failed to melt since the Ice Age.

It was a harsh place. Few plants could survive the combination of the summer's shallow thawed-out soil and the intensely bitter winds of winter. But now, on the ground, from under the melting snow, the frozen world was coming to life.

Dead-looking stems bore tiny leaves and flowers, and the land was peppered with green and white and yellow. The first insects were stirring too. There were flies in the air, and some spiders and mites toiling on the ground. Silverhair saw a caterpillar cocoon fixed to a dwarf willow. The cocoon twitched as if its occupant were impatient to begin life's brief adventure.

The edges of the receding snow patches were busy places. New arrivals – migrant birds like buntings, sanderling, turnstone and horned larks – rushed to and fro, as if in desperation, as the sun revealed fresh land with its cargo of roots and insects, ripe for the eating. The noise of the birds was startling after the long silence of the winter.

The lemmings seemed plentiful this year. Their heads popped up everywhere from their holes in the snow, and in some places their busy teeth had already denuded the land, leaving the characteristic 'lemming carpet' of shorn grass and hard black droppings.

And the lemming hunters were here too. As soon as any lemming left its ball-shaped nest, a long-tailed skua would take off after it, yelping display calls emanating from its hooked beak.

Usually the hapless rodents became nothing more than gifts in a skua's courtship display. But Silverhair saw one enterprising animal, attacked by a skua, rear up on its hind legs and flash its long teeth. The skua, alarmed, flew away, and Silverhair felt obscurely cheered. She could hear the clattering heartbeat of the little creature, as it nibbled in peace at a blade of grass.

But it was probably only a brief respite. The lemmings were hunted ruthlessly, not just by the skuas, but by snowy owls, gulls and buzzards, and even Arctic foxes and polar bears. Silverhair knew that this lemming's life, compared to her own, would be fast, vivid, but – even if by some miracle the predators spared it – tragically short.

The sun completed many rounds in the sky as the two mammoths walked on.

Wolfnose even brought Silverhair to some richer pastures, urging her to remember them for the future. 'And,' she said, 'you must understand why the grass grows so well here.'

'Why?'

'Once there were many mammoths here – many Families, many Clans. And they had favourite pastures, where their dung would be piled thick. The Clans are gone now – all save ours – but, even after so long, their dung enriches the Earth . . .'

Silverhair stared with awe at the thick-growing grass, a vibrant memorial to the great mammoth herds of long ago.

They came at last to the western coast.

The sea was still largely frozen. Sanderling and bunting searched for seeds in the snow, ducks dived through narrow leads in the thin ice, and skuas stood expectantly on prominent rocks. On the cliff below, barnacle geese were already incubating their clutches of eggs, still surrounded by the brilliant white of snow.

The smells of salt water and guano were all but overpowering. But it was here that the stink of rotten mammoth flesh was strongest of all, and Silverhair was filled with a powerful dread.

At last they came to a shallow, rounded hill. Silverhair could see that it had been badly eroded by recent rainstorms; deep gullies ran down its side, as if scored there by giant tusks.

Wolfnose edged forward, and poked at the ground with her trunk. 'This is called a *yedoma*,' she said. 'It is a hill mostly made of ice. Come now.'

She led Silverhair around the flank of the hill. The death stink grew steadily stronger, until Silverhair could hardly bear to take another step. But Wolfnose marched stolidly on, her trunk raised, and Silverhair had no option but to follow.

And they came to a place where the *yedoma*'s collapsing flank had exposed a corpse: the corpse of a mammoth.

Wolfnose stood back, her trunk raised. 'Tell me what you see, little Silverhair,' she said gently.

Silverhair, shocked and distressed, stepped forward slowly, nosing at the ground with her trunk. 'I think it was a Bull . . .'

The dead mammoth was lying on his side. Silverhair could see that the flesh and skin on which he lay were mostly intact: she could make out his ear on that side, his flank, the skin on his legs, the long dark hair of winter tangled in frozen mud.

But the upper side of the Bull had been stripped of its flesh, by the sharp teeth of scavengers. The meat was almost completely removed from the skull, and the ribcage, and even the legs. There was no sign of the Bull's trunk. The pelvis, shoulder blade and several of the ribs were broken and scattered. Inside the ribcage nestled a dark, lumpy mass, still frozen hard; perhaps it was the heart and stomach of this dead mammoth.

The Bull, she found, still had traces of food in the ruin of his mouth: grass and sedge, just as she had eaten today. He must have died rapidly, then: too rapidly even to swallow his last meal.

The flensed skull gleamed white in the pale sunlight. Its empty eye socket seemed to stare at her accusingly.

She heard a soft growl. She turned, trumpeting.

A wolf stood there, its fur white as snow. It was a bitch; Silverhair could see swollen dugs dangling beneath her chest.

Silverhair lowered her head, trumpeted again, and lunged at the wolf. 'Get away, cub of Aglu, or I will drive my tusks into you!'

The wolf dropped her ears and ran off.

Silverhair, breathing hard, returned to Wolfnose. 'If she returns, I will kill her.'

Wolfnose said, 'No. She has her place, as we all do. She probably has cubs to feed.'

'She has been chewing on the corpse of this Bull!'

Wolfnose trumpeted mockingly. 'And what difference does that make to him now? He has belonged to the wolves for a long time: in fact, longer than you think, little Silverhair . . .'

Silverhair returned to her inspection of the ravaged corpse. 'I don't recognise him. He must be from a Family I never met.'

'You don't understand yet,' Wolfnose said gently. 'Perhaps he was grazing at the soft edge of a gully or a river bluff. Perhaps he lost his footing, became trapped. The wolves would work at him, and in time he would die. But then, at last, he would be enveloped by the soil, saturated by water, frozen by winter's return.

'But the river mud that destroyed him also preserved him.

'For you see, if your body happens to be sealed inside ice, it can be saved. The ice, freezing, draws out the moisture that would otherwise rot your flesh . . . If you were sealed here, Silverhair, although your spirit would long have flown to the aurora, your body would live on – as long as it remained inside the ice, it would be as well preserved as this.'

'*How long?*'

Wolfnose said, 'I don't know. How can I know? Perhaps Great-Years. Perhaps longer . . .'

Silverhair was stunned.

She could reach down with her trunk and touch the hair of this Bull's face. The Bull might have been dead only a few days. And yet – could it be true? – he was separated from her by Great-Years.

'Now,' said Wolfnose. 'Look with new eyes; lift your trunk and *smell* . . .'

Silverhair, a little bewildered, obeyed.

And, now that her eyes and nostrils were accustomed to the stink of the ancient corpse beside her, she saw that this landscape was not as it had seemed.

It was littered with bones.

Here was a femur, a leg-bone, thrusting defiantly from the ground. Here was a set of ribs, broken and scattered, split as if some scavenger had been working to extract the marrow from their cores. And there a skull protruded from the ground, as if some great beast were burrowing upwards from within the Earth.

Wolfnose said, 'The bones and bodies are stored in the ground. But when the ice melts and they are exposed – after Great-Years of stillness and dark – there is a moment of daylight, a flash of activity. The wolves and birds soon come to take away the flesh, and the bones are scattered by the wind and the rain. And then it is done. The ancient bodies evaporate like a grain of snow on the tongue. So you see, you are fortunate to have witnessed this rare moment of surfacing, Silverhair.'

'We should Remember the one in the *yedoma*,' she said.

'Of course we should,' said Wolfnose. 'For he has no one left to do it for him.'

And so the two mammoths touched the vacant skull with their trunks, and lifted and sorted the bones. Then they gathered twigs and soil and cast it on the ancient corpse, and touched it with the sensitive pads of their back feet, and they stood over it as the sun wheeled around the sky. They were trying to Remember the spirit which had once occupied this body, this Bull with no name who might have been an ancestor of them both, just as they would have done had they come upon the body of one of their own Family.

Silverhair imagined the days of long ago – perhaps when the crushed corpse she had seen had been proud and full of life – days different from now, days when the Clan had covered the Island, days when Families had merged and mingled in the great migrations like rivers flowing together. Days when mammoths had been more numerous, on the Island and beyond, than pebbles on a beach.

She was standing on a ground filled with the bodies of mammoths, generations of them stretching back Great-Years and more, bodies that were raised to the surface, to glimmer in the sun and evaporate like dew. For the first time in her life she could *see* the great depth of mammoth history behind her: forty million years of it, stretching back to Kilukpuk herself in her Swamp, a great sweep of time and space of which she was just a part.

Like the bones of this long-dead Bull, her soul was merely the fragment of all that mystery which happened to have surfaced in the here and now. And like the Bull, her soul would be worn away and vanish in an instant.

Silverhair felt the world shift and flow around her, as if she herself were caught up by some great river of time.

And she was proud, fiercely proud, to be mammoth.

When they were done, the two mammoths turned away from the setting sun, side by side, and prepared for the long walk back to their Family.

At the last moment, Wolfnose stopped and turned back. 'Silverhair – what of the tusks?'

Somehow Silverhair had not noticed the Bull's tusks, one way or another. She trotted back to the *yedoma*.

The tusks had not been snapped away by whatever accident had befallen this Bull, for the stumps in the skull were sharply terminated, in clean, flat edges. And the tusks themselves were missing; there was no sign of them, not so much as a splinter.

She returned to Wolfnose and told her this.

For the first time, she detected fear in the voice of the old one. 'Then the Lost have been here.'

'*What?*'

'I know what you saw on the ice floe in the south, little Silverhair,' Wolfnose said gravely. 'Perhaps they came in search of flesh, like the wolf . . .'

'What do the Lost want with tusks?'

'There is no understanding the Lost,' said Wolfnose bluntly. 'There is only fleeing. Come. Let us return to Owlheart and the others.'

Their shadows stretching ahead of them, the two mammoths walked together.

Chapter Two

THE HOLE GOUGED OUT OF THE SKY

Silverhair was impatient during the long journey back to the Family.

It struck her as a paradox that visiting a place of death and desolation like the Plain of Bones should leave her feeling so invigorated. But that was how she felt – as Wolfnose had surely intended.

And – besides all the philosophy – she was *young*, and the days of spring were bright and warming, and the tundra flowers were already starting to bloom, bright yellow amid the last scraps of snow and the first green shoots of new grass. Just as the Cycle promised, she felt as if she was shedding her cares with the worn-out layers of her winter coat.

Perhaps it would be this year that she would, for the first time, sing the Song of Oestrus: when her body would produce the eggs that could form a calf. She remembered the ache in her empty dugs as she had watched Foxeye suckle Sunfire for the first time. Now she could feel the blood surge in her veins, as if drawn by the sun.

She wanted to become pregnant: to bear her own calf, to shelter and feed and raise it, to teach it all she knew of the world, to add her own new thread to the Cycle's great and unending coat.

And her thoughts were full of Lop-ear. She longed to tell him what she had seen on the Plain of Bones, what it had meant to her . . .

She longed, bluntly, just to be with him once more.

She trotted across the thawing plains, her head full of warm, blood-red dreams of the young Bull.

Wolfnose had more difficulty.

Even at the best of times her pace was no match for Silverhair's. The pain in her legs and back was obvious. It took her much longer than Silverhair to feed and to pass dung, and her lengthening stops left Silverhair fretting with impatience.

Thus they proceeded, Wolfnose warring with her own failing body, Silverhair torn between eagerness for the future and responsibility for the past.

At last they came in sight of the Family.

It was a bright morning, and at the centre of a greening plain, the Family looked like a series of round, hairy boulders, dotted over the landscape. The smell of their dung and their moist coats was already strong, and Silverhair could feel the rumble of their voices as they called to each other. The mammoths were not beautiful – never had the ambiguous gift of great Matriarch Ganesha to her daughter Prima been more evident to Silverhair – but it was, in her eyes, the finest sight she could have seen.

She raised her trunk and trumpeted her joyous greeting, and – quite forgetting Wolfnose – she charged across the tundra towards the Family.

Here came Lop-ear, that damaged ear dangling unmistakably by his head, running to meet her.

Their meeting was so vigorous she was almost knocked over.

They bumped their foreheads, ran in circles, defecated together and spun around. He was like a reflection in a meltpond, a reflection of her own resurgent youth and vigour. This is our time, she thought as she spun and danced; this is our summer, our day.

And it seemed perfectly natural that he should run behind her, rear up on his hind legs, place his forelegs on her back, and rest his great weight against her.

But she was not in oestrus, and he was not in musth, and – for now – the mounting was only a playful celebration.

They faced each other; Silverhair touched his scalp and tusks and mouth.

'I missed you,' he said.

'And I you. You won't believe what Wolfnose showed me—' And she began to recount all she had seen in the Plain of Bones, the ancient carcasses of mammoths just like themselves, swimming out of the ice after a Great-Year's sleep.

But, though he listened intently, and continued to stroke her trunk with his, she could see that his eyes were empty.

After a time she drew back from him. He reached for her again, but she pushed him gently away.

'Something's wrong. Is it what Owlheart said, about having something of the Lost in you?'

'No. Or at least, not just that. I'm confused, Silverhair. I'm happy to see you, glad the spring has come again. Part of me wants to jump about like a calf. But inside, I feel as if a giant black winter cloud is hanging over me.'

She scuffed at the ground, trying to retain that sense of wondrous optimism with which she had returned home. 'I don't understand—'

'Silverhair, if you were singing the Song of Oestrus now – *who would mount you?*'

And with that question she saw his concern. For there were

only two Bulls here who might come into musth: Eggtusk and Lop-ear. They'd fought once already; they might easily kill each other fighting over her.

Or over Owlheart, or Foxeye, or even Snagtooth, if their turn came.

Lop-ear said, 'And even if we resolve our dominance fights without killing each other – even if all the Cows become pregnant by one or other of us – what then?'

'What do you mean?'

'What of the future? When Sunfire and Croptail and any other calves grow up – and themselves come into oestrus and musth – who is to mate with *them*?' He spun, agitated, his trunk raised as if to ward off invisible enemies. 'Already his mother is pushing Croptail away. That's as it should be. Soon, in a few years, he will want to leave the Family and search for other Bulls, join a bachelor herd. Just as I did, just as Eggtusk did. But Croptail *can't* join the Bulls, for there *are* no other Bulls. He can't join a bachelor herd, for there *is* no herd – none that we have met for a long time, at any rate. And when he is in musth, there will be no Cows but his own sisters and aunts and cousins.'

She reached out to try to calm him. 'Lop-ear—'

But he spun away from her. 'Oh, Kilukpuk! I have this stuff rattling around in my skull all day and all night. I want to stop thinking!'

She was chilled by his words, even as she strove to understand. To think so clearly about the possibilities of the future, of change, is not common in mammoths; embedded in the great rhythms of time, they live in the here and now. But Lop-ear was no ordinary mammoth.

She took hold of his trunk and forced him to face her. 'Lop-ear – listen to me. Perhaps you're right, in all you say. But you are wrong to despair. When we were trapped by the fire and the runoff you found a way to save us. It wasn't a teaching from the Cycle; it wasn't something the Matriarch showed you. It was a new idea.

'Now we are facing a barrier even more formidable than that stream. There is nothing to guide us in the Cycle. There is nothing the Matriarch can advise us to do. *It's up to us*, Lop-ear. We have to seek out the new, and find a way to survive.'

'It's impossible.'

'No. As Longtusk said, *only death is the end of possibility*. What we must do is look for answers where nobody has looked before.'

'Where?'

She hesitated, and the vague determination that had long been gathering in her crystallised. 'If Eggtusk is right – that the Lost have come to this Island – then that's where we must go.'

'*The Lost?* Silverhair, are you rogue?'

'No. Just determined. Maybe the Lost aren't the monsters of the Cycle any more. Maybe there's some way they can help us.' She tightened her grasp on his trunk. 'We must go south again. Are you with me?'

For long heartbeats, he stared into her eyes. Then he said: 'Yes. Oh, Silverhair, yes. I'll follow you to the End of the World—'

There was an alarmed trumpeting.

Silverhair released Lop-ear's trunk and they both whirled, trunks held aloft.

Owlheart was running. 'Wolfnose! Wolfnose!'

Silverhair looked back to the west, the way she had come.

Wolfnose, trailing Silverhair's footsteps, had fallen to her knees.

Her heart surging, Silverhair ran after her Matriarch.

*

Silverhair, driven by guilt, was the first to reach Wolfnose.

The old Cow's belly and chest were resting against the ground, her legs splayed, and her trunk was pooled before her. Shanks of winter fur were scattered around her. Her eyes were closed, and it seemed to Silverhair as if she were slowly subsiding, as if the blood and life were leaking out of her into the hard ground.

She reached out and ran her trunk over the old Cow's face. The skin looked as rough as bark, but it was warm and soft to the touch, and she could hear the soft gurgle of Wolfnose's breathing.

Wolfnose opened her eyes. They were sunk in pools of black, wrinkled skin. 'Oh, little Silverhair,' she said softly.

'Are you tired?'

'Oh, yes. And hungry, so hungry. Perhaps I'll sleep now, and then feed a little more . . .'

She started to tip over.

Silverhair rushed to Wolfnose's side. Wolfnose's great weight settled against her flank, slack and lifeless, and Silverhair staggered, barely able to support her.

But now the others were here: Lop-ear, Owlheart and Eggtusk. Silverhair saw that Owlheart had, with remarkable calm and foresight, carried a trunkful of water with her. She offered dribbles of it to Wolfnose, and Silverhair saw Wolfnose's pink, cracked tongue uncurl and lap at the cool, clear liquid.

Wolfnose's eyes flickered open once more. She raised her trunk, so heavy it looked as if it were stuffed with river mud, and laid it over Owlheart's scalp. 'You're a good daughter, Grassfoot . . .'

The Matriarch said, 'I'll be a better one when you're on your feet again.'

Wolfnose shuddered, and a deep, ominous gurgling sounded from her lungs. Silverhair listened in horror; it was as if something had broken inside Wolfnose.

Wolfnose closed her eyes once more, and her trunk fell away from Owlheart's head.

Owlheart stepped back, staring at her mother in dismay.

When Eggtusk saw that Owlheart was giving up, he roared defiance. 'By Kilukpuk's piss-soaked hind leg, you're not done yet, Cow!'

He ran around Wolfnose, and pushed his head between her slack buttocks. Then he dug his heels into the ground and heaved. The massive body rocked. Eggtusk looked up and bellowed to Silverhair and Lop-ear: 'Come on, you lazy calves. Don't just stand there. Push!'

Lop-ear and Silverhair glanced at each other. Then they braced themselves and pushed at Wolfnose's sides.

Even after the trials of the winter – during which she had shed more fat than was good for her – Wolfnose was a mature Cow, and very heavy. Silverhair could feel Wolfnose's ribs grinding as they shoved the slack body upwards.

But, between them, they managed to lift her off the ground. Wolfnose's legs straightened out, like cracking tree branches, and her feet settled on the ground.

'That's it!' Eggtusk bellowed. 'Hold her now!'

But there was no strength in those old legs. Silverhair staggered sideways, as Wolfnose's bulk slid against her body.

Eggtusk cried out, 'No!'

But it was too late. Wolfnose slumped to the ground, this time falling on her side.

Eggtusk began pushing at Wolfnose's buttocks once more. 'Come on! Help me, you dung-heaps! Help me . . .' But Wolfnose could not stand again.

Eggtusk crashed to his knees before her. Wolfnose's eyes,

flickering open and closed, swivelled towards him. Eggtusk lifted her limp trunk on to his tusks. Draping the trunk over his head, he put his own trunk into her mouth.

A watching human would have been startled by the familiarity of his choking cries, and the heaving of his chest.

This was love, Silverhair thought, awed. A love of an intensity and depth and timelessness she had never imagined possible. She knew that she would be privileged if, during her life, she ever received or gave such devotion.

And she had never suspected it existed between Eggtusk and Wolfnose.

But Owlheart came to him now. 'No more, Eggtusk.' And Owlheart wrapped her trunk around his face.

Lop-ear was at Silverhair's side.

'Oh, Lop-ear,' Silverhair said, and her own vision blurred as flat salty tears welled in her eyes. 'If she hadn't walked with me all that way to the Plain of Bones – if I hadn't been so careless as to rush her back, to leave her behind so thoughtlessly . . . All I wanted was to get back, and—'

'Hush,' he said. 'She wanted to take you to the Plain.'

'I could have said no—'

'And treat her with disrespect? She wouldn't have wanted that. It's nobody's fault. It is her time.' And he twined his trunk in hers, and held her still.

Wolfnose lifted her trunk, shuddered, and slumped. Her breath sighed out of her in a long growl, like a final contact rumble.

Then she was still.

Eggtusk rocked over Wolfnose. He nudged her head with his. He placed his trunk in her mouth again, and her trunk in his, and intertwined their trunks. He even walked around behind her and placed his forelegs on her back, as if he were trying to mount her. And he raised his trunk and trumpeted his distress to the empty lands.

Before the end of the day, Owlheart led all the Family to Wolfnose's body for the Remembering. The sun was low now and it painted the Earth with gold and fire. Eggtusk, his trunk drooping as he stood over the body, was a noble shadow in Silverhair's eyes, the stiff hairs of his back catching the liquid light.

The calves were both staring at the body. Little Sunfire's trunk was raised in alarm.

Foxeye tapped at the calves with her trunk. 'Watch now,' she said, 'and learn. This is how to die.'

Silverhair found herself staring too. The loss she felt was enormous, as if a hole had been gouged out of the sky.

Owlheart stepped forward, and scraped at the bare ground with her tusks. Then she picked up a fingerful of earth and grass and dropped it on Wolfnose's unresponding flank.

Silverhair reached down, ripped up some grass, and stepped forward to do the same.

Soon all the Family were following Owlheart's lead, covering Wolfnose's body with mud, earth, grass and twigs. Eggtusk kicked and scraped at the soil, sending heaps of it over the carcass. Even the calves tried to help; little Sunfire looked comical as she tottered back and forth to the fallen body with a blade of grass or a scrap of dust.

As they worked, Silverhair felt a deeper calm settle on her soul. The Cycle said this was how the mammoths – and their Cousins, the Calves of Probos, the world over – had always honoured and remembered their dead. Now Silverhair felt the ancient truth and wisdom of the ceremonial seep into her. It was a way to show their love for the spark of Wolfnose, as it floated across the river of darkness to the aurora, leaving the daylight diminished.

When they were done, the mammoths stood a little longer over the body, and wove restlessly from side to side, the younger ones joining in without thinking.

Then Owlheart turned away, and quoted a final line from the Cycle: '*She belongs to the wolves now.*'

She led the Family away. Eggtusk walked at her side, still desolate, his trunk dangling limp between his legs.

Silverhair looked back once. The mound of Wolfnose's body looked like the *yedoma* within which she had seen the emerging, ancient corpse.

Suddenly she saw this scene as it might be Great-Years from now. She saw another mammoth, young and foolish as herself, come lumbering across the plain – to discover Wolfnose's body, stripped by time of flesh and name, emerging once more from the icy ground. It was like a vision of her own life, she thought: as intense as sunlight, as brief as the glimmer of hoar-frost.

She sought out Lop-ear. She stroked his musth gland with her trunk, but he shrank back, oddly.

She turned her face towards the south.

He hesitated. 'Now?'

'Yes. Now.'

'. . . Shouldn't we tell the others?'

'What for? They would only stop us.'

She began to walk. Resolutely, she did not look back.

After a few heartbeats she heard his heavy footfalls as he lumbered after her. She hid her grim satisfaction.

Chapter Three

THE TIME OF MUSTH AND OESTRUS

Once more, their walk took them many days.

They passed through a valley flanked by eroded mountains.

It was a valley of water and light. Gently undulating meadows fell away to a central river, which was slow-moving, wide and deep, meandering through a sandy flood-plain. To the west the river's numerous tangled channels shimmered in the low sun. Above them the valley sides rose up to become dramatic peaks, the white light blazing off the ice that crowned them. The basalt walls, their sheer rock faces shattered by centuries of frost, had eroded into narrow pinnacles that stood against the sky. Every ledge was coated with orange lichen, nourished by the droppings of geese, whose cackling calls echoed down to the mammoths.

There was little snow left on the valley floor now, and trickles of water, cool and fresh, ran from the remaining snow banks. But the ground was still bare, shaded rust-red, ochre and russet; of the lush vegetation which would soon cover the valley there was still little sign.

The first bumble bees and butterflies were appearing in the air.

Silverhair suffered her first mosquito bite of the year. She snapped at the troublesome insect with her tail, but she knew that even if she reached it her effort was futile; millions of its relatives would soon be emerging from the silt at the bottom of ice-covered ponds, where they had spent the winter as larvae.

The beauty of the valley, the return of life, the calmness of their situation: all of this, as the long days wore on, was having a profound effect on Silverhair. She could feel the flesh and fat gathering comfortably on her bones, her winter coat falling away. And her body responded deeply to the season, surging with oceanic warmth.

Somewhere within her, seeds were ripening, as if in response to the death she had witnessed. It was oestrus; she was thrilled.

And she knew that Lop-ear, too, was ready. As he walked he kept his head held high, his trunk curled. He seethed with irritability and urgency. He dribbled musth from the temporal gland at the top of his head, and he left a trail of strong-smelling urine wherever he walked. He was even making a deep rumble, a sound she had only heard from much older Bulls before. But he seemed consumed by his own inner turmoil and ill-defined longing, and when he spoke to her it was only of their greater concerns: the strange encounter with the Lost that might await them in the south, the possibility of bringing the Family to these richer lands, the disturbing, nagging fact that they were finding no recent signs of other mammoth Families anywhere.

He spoke of everything but *them*.

He was in musth.

And yet he couldn't see it himself.

Patiently, she kept her counsel and waited for him to understand.

After many days of walking, they came to a ridge that overlooked the southern coast of the Island.

The world to the south lay displayed before Silverhair, divided into broad stripes, dazzling in her poor vision. Below the blue-grey line of sky there was the misty bulk of the Mainland, still obscured by storm cloud. Then came the Channel, a blue-black strip of water fringed by cracked, gleaming pack ice. Below the ridge they were standing on was the shore, a shingle beach fringed by dirty landfast ice.

The all-pervasive sound rising from the coast was of broken pack ice lifting on and off the shore rocks. Further away, in the open Channel, icebergs drifted: a procession of them, mysterious and awe-inspiring, like clouds brought down to Earth. As the light shifted, their contours would suddenly glow iridescent blue. Silverhair's heart was lifted by the stately beauty and strangeness of the bergs; they were the mammoths of the sea, she thought, effortlessly dominating their surroundings, giant and dignified.

The wind here was strong, and its cold penetrated Silverhair's newly exposed underwool. She huddled close to Lop-ear, the wind whipping across her eyes. 'There are times when I wish I could keep my winter fur all year around—'

'Hush,' he said, staring. '*Look.*'

. . . And there, resting on the shore, was something she had never seen before.

At first she thought it was the splayed-open body of some giant animal. It had one end coming to a point, the other rounded. Its long, sleek flanks were encrusted with sea plants and streaks of brownish discoloration. And those flanks were torn open, she saw, perhaps ripped by the sea ice. The top of the monster was like a complex, shattered forest, with posts like tree-trunks sprouting from each other at all angles.

The thing was huge: so big she could have walked around inside its belly.

Lop-ear was silent, staring at the hulk, his trunk raised in the air.

Silverhair said, 'Do you think it's dead?'

'I don't think it was ever alive,' he said bluntly.

'What, then?'

'I think you must ask the Lost that,' he said. 'For something as ugly and unfitting as *that* could only come from their tortured souls. Perhaps it brought them here.'

'But it's damaged. Perhaps that's why they can't leave.' Suddenly she raised her trunk. 'I smell something.'

'Yes.' He turned, scanning along the coast.

It was smoke.

They saw a small fire, confined to a spot on the beach below, close to the foot of the ridge. There was, Silverhair saw, a shape above it: like a tree, bent all the way over to touch the ground. There were objects dangling from the tree-thing, over the fire.

Now she could smell something else, carried on the wind. The stink of burning flesh.

And that bent-over object wasn't a tree, she realised with mounting horror.

It was a tusk.

'By Kilukpuk's mercy . . .'

Lop-ear was becoming agitated. 'That smell of flesh—' His voice was tight and indistinct. 'It is all I can do to keep from fleeing.'

'Lop-ear, listen to me.' She told him about the body in the *yedoma*. The way the tusks of the ancient Bull had been hacked away. 'Well, now I know what became of those tusks,' she said grimly.

Now there was movement on the beach. Two creatures – something like wolves, perhaps, but walking upright, on their hind legs – approached the fire. One of them reached out with its foreleg and prodded at the dangling scraps of flesh. It was using its paw as Silverhair would her trunk, to manipulate the burned flesh.

To rip a piece off it.

To lift it to its mouth, and bite into it. Another of the creatures grabbed at the meat, and they fought over it, clumsily.

She felt bile rise in her own throat.

Without speaking, the two mammoths turned and fled from the ridge, towards the sanctity and calmness of the north.

The sun rolled along the mist-shrouded horizon. The Moon rose, a gaunt old crescent, clearly visible in the mysterious, subdued sky of the summer midnight.

The two mammoths huddled together.

'They were Lost,' Silverhair whispered. 'Weren't they? How can I have ever imagined I could deal with them?' Every instinct, every nerve shrieked for her to fly from this place, from the Lost and their scentless, unnatural activities, their slavering like wolves over burned scraps of flesh.

But Lop-ear didn't reply.

By the wan light she could see him, apparently unconsciously, reaching into his mouth with his trunk, and tasting her musk. Tasting it for oestrus.

Suddenly it was not a time for talking. And her fear, in this strange, remote place, her residual sadness at Wolfnose's death – all of it transmuted into a powerful longing.

She rumbled, deeper and lower than ever in her life. Then her tone rose gently, becoming stronger and higher in pitch, and sinking down to silence at the end.

This was the Song of Oestrus. The call would carry many days' walk from here, and was a signal to any Bull who heard it that she was a Cow ready to mate.

But there was only one Bull she wanted to hear.

She pulled away from Lop-ear, her head held high. Then she whirled around, backing into him.

She ran across the shadow-strewn plain, the frosty grass crushing beneath her feet, her breath steaming before her face. She could feel him pursuing her, his own giant footfalls like an echo of her own – but much more than an echo, for as he neared her it was as if the other half of her own soul was joining her.

She let him catch her.

He laid his trunk over her shoulder, pulling her back. Still singing, she turned to face him. He was silhouetted in the low light, his body, newly fattened by the spring grass, broad and strong. She stepped from side to side, slowly, and every step she took was mirrored by him. She could see the musth liquid which oozed thickly from the gland on top of his head.

Then, facing her, he gently laid his trunk on her head and body. She twined her trunk around his, and their mouths met.

Thus, since the time of Probos, have mammoths and their Cousins expressed their readiness to mate.

Now, at last, she let him move behind her.

He placed his tusks and forelegs on her back, and raised himself up. She knew he was taking most of his weight on his own back legs, but even so his mass was solid, heavy, warm on her back.

And she felt him enter her.

When it was over, and his warmth was captured inside her, she entered the mating pandemonium. She rumbled, screamed, trumpeted, defecated, secreted from her musth gland, whirled in a dance that made the ground shake. If other

Cows were here they would have joined in with Silverhair's pandemonium now, celebrating the deep ancient joy of the mating. It was as if all her experiences – of death and birth and renewed life, of the immense mammoth history which lay behind her – channelled through this moment. The blood surged in her, remaking her like a larva in its cocoon, and she knew she had never been so alive, so joyous, so tied to the Earth.

This was her summer day; this was her moment. She trumpeted her defiant joy that she was *alive*.

And at that moment of greatest joy she saw, climbing high in the midnight sky, a splinter of red light: it was the Sky Steppe, where one day her calves would roam free and without fear.

Afterwards they stood together, their hides matted, their heads touching.

'You know I will stay with you,' he said. 'I will guard you from the other Bulls until the end of your oestrus.'

That was the way, she knew. Mammoths are not romantic, but Lop-ear would protect his mate until the end of her oestrus period, when – she hoped – conception would occur, deep within her. Still, she could not help but mock him. '*What* other Bulls?'

'I will defend you even from the great Bull Croptail!' He raised his head, so his tusks flashed in the flat sunlight, and he danced before her as if he were about to go into battle with the Earth itself—

There was a sharp sound behind them. A cracking twig.

Mammoths' necks are short, and they cannot easily turn their heads. So Silverhair and Lop-ear lumbered about, to face behind them.

There was something here, just paces away. Like a narrow,

branchless tree, casting a long midnight shadow. Silverhair could smell nothing of it.

It was a Lost.

Now it moved. With raised forelegs it lifted some kind of stick, and pointed it at them.

Lop-ear said, 'We must not show it fear. And we must not frighten it. It is only a Hotblood, like us, after all.' He hesitated. 'Perhaps it is injured. Perhaps it is hungry. That might be the meaning of the stick it carries—'

Dread filled her. 'Lop-ear, don't!'

'It's what we have come for, Silverhair.'

Lop-ear lowered his trunk, and stepped forward. From his forehead resounded the contact rumble.

The apparition took a step back, raised its stick higher. And the stick cracked.

There was a burst of light, a sound like thunder.

It was over in an instant. But that crack of light was enough to show her the strange, hairless head of the creature before her. It was the one she had met on the ice floe: the one she had called Skin-of-Ice.

Lop-ear was trumpeting in pain. She turned.

His trunk was raised, his eyes closed. And some dark liquid was gushing over the fur on his chest. It was blood, and it steamed in the cold air.

His hind legs gave way, so that he squatted like a defecating wolf, and his trunk dropped.

She raced to his side. 'What has happened to you?'

But he could not speak. Now blood spewed from his open mouth, dangling in loops from his tongue.

She ran behind him, and began to nudge at his back with her head. 'Get up! Get up!'

He tried; she could feel him padding at the ground with his hind legs, and he lifted his head.

But there was another thunder crack.

Immediately all four of Lop-ear's legs gave way and he slumped to the ground.

Silverhair staggered back, appalled, terrified. She could not understand what was happening. But she still had Lop-ear's warmth inside her, and she was drawn back to him.

There was a new sound now: a thin, high whoop, almost like a calf's immature trumpeting.

It was the creature called Skin-of-Ice, she saw. It – *he* – was holding his thunder-stick in the air above his head, and was yelping out his triumph. And he was standing on the flank of fallen Lop-ear.

Silverhair felt rage gather in her, deep and uncontrollable. She raised herself up on her hind legs, head high, and trumpeted as loudly as she could.

Skin-of-Ice raised the thunder-stick, and it cracked, again and again. Stinging, invisible insects flew around her.

Her mind crumbled into panic, and she fled.

Later, she would remember little of what followed. Only flashes, like the light from Skin-of-Ice's thunder-stick.

Sometimes she was alone, fleeing across a shadowed plain.

Sometimes the Lost pursued her, thin legs working, mysterious thunder-sticks barking.

Sometimes Lop-ear was here. She spoke to him of the future, the plans they had made. She threatened him with the punishment he would receive from Eggtusk if he didn't get up and come with her back to the Family right now.

Sometimes she saw a caterpillar, motionless on a willow branch. Then a small opening in its moist hide revealed a set of jaws: it was a larva of some still smaller insect, eating its host alive from within.

Sometimes there was only the stink of Lop-ear's cooling blood in her nostrils.

And always, always, the image of Skin-of-Ice: how the murderous Lost would look when she raised his soft, worm-like body on the tip of her tusks.

Chapter Four

THE RHYTHMS AND THE LOST

The sun wheeled above the horizon, never setting; the endless daylight was pitiless, for Silverhair sought only darkness.

'Silverhair. Silverhair . . .'

The words were like contact rumbles, swimming through the earth. And when she opened her eyes, unrolled her trunk so she could smell again, she could see mammoths before her: Eggtusk, Snagtooth.

With a part of her mind she knew that she had tried to find her way north, back to the Family, where they remained on the bleak plain of volcanic rock in the lee of the great Mountains at the End of the World. She recalled the walk in only fragmented glimpses: the clumps of grass she had once grazed with Lop-ear, an old hill whose eroded contours had reminded her of Lop-ear's slumped carcass.

She tried to focus on Eggtusk's words. '. . . You must listen to what I'm saying. I understand how you feel. We all do. But death is waiting for each of us. The great turning of life and death . . .'

But then the mammoths would float away from her again, like woolly clouds.

'It was the Lost,' Silverhair mumbled. 'The Lost and his thunder-stick—'

But they wouldn't listen. 'Even the Lost are part of the Cycle,' said Eggtusk. 'Though they don't know it. We are not like the Lost. Give yourself up to the Cycle, little Silverhair. Close your eyes . . .'

Silverhair felt the rocks under her feet, as if her legs were burrowing like tree-trunks to anchor her to the ground which sustained them all. And, slowly, the Cycle's calm teaching reached her.

She remembered how Wolfnose had shown her the Plain of Bones. She felt the great turning rhythms of the Earth. Her mind opened up, as if she held the topology of the whole Earth in her mind, and she saw far beyond the now, to the farthest reaches of past and future.

Her own long life, in the midst of all that epic sweep, was no more than the brief spring blossoming of a tundra flower. And Lop-ear, the same. *And yet they mattered:* just as each flower contributed to the waves of white and gold which swept across the tundra, so she and Lop-ear were inextricable parts of the great whole.

And the most important thing in the whole world was Lop-ear's warmth in her belly: the possibility, still, that she might conceive his calf.

'. . . To the Lost there is only the here and now,' Eggtusk was saying. 'They are a young species – a couple of Great-Years, no more – while we are ancient. They have no Cycle. They are just sparks of mind, isolated and frightened and soon extinguished. They never hear the greater rhythms, and never find their place in the world. That is why they disturb so much of what they touch. They are trying to forget what they are. They are dancing in the face of oblivion . . .'

Silverhair raised her head. She could feel the salt tears brim in her eyes. 'But it was my fault.'

'Lop-ear was much smarter than you are,' Eggtusk said gently. 'You couldn't have made him do anything he didn't want to do. Even *I* couldn't, and I fought him to prove the point – much as I regret that now, by Kilukpuk's cracked and festering nipples!'

'But I didn't even perform the Remembering for him.'

'No. Well, we can't very well leave him like that.' Eggtusk laid his trunk on her head, and scratched behind her ear. 'Do you know where you are?'

She looked around, at featureless tundra. 'No,' she admitted.

'You're far from the Family. Far from anywhere. You've been wandering, Silverhair. Wandering, but not eating by the look of you. When you didn't return, Owlheart sent me to find you. It wasn't easy.'

'I – thank you, Eggtusk.'

'Never mind that. You must eat and sleep, young Silverhair. For we have a walk ahead of us. Back to the south.'

For the first time since she had lost Lop-ear, her spirits lifted. 'To Lop-ear.'

'Yes.'

'I'm surprised Owlheart let you go.'

'I had to promise we'd come back in one piece. Oh, and—'

'Yes?'

He bent so only she could hear. 'I had to take Snagtooth with me.'

The three mammoths set off at midnight. There was a layer of cloud above, but the pale-orange sun hung above the horizon in a clear strip of sky.

Heading south, the mammoths walked slowly, frequently pausing to pass dung and feed. Despite Silverhair's urgent wish to return to Lop-ear's bones, Eggtusk insisted they eat their fill. They were coming into the richest season of the year, the time when the mammoths must lay in their reserves of fat, without which they cannot survive the next winter. As Eggtusk said to Silverhair, 'I'd lick out the crusty lichen from between Kilukpuk's pus-ridden toes before I'd let you starve yourself to death. What use would that be to Lop-ear, or any of us? Eh?'

And so, under his coaxing and scolding, she cropped the grass and flowers, and the fresh buds of the dwarf willows whose branches barely grew high enough to cover her toes.

Snagtooth continued to be a problem. A growing one, in fact.

Though the stump of her smashed tusk had healed over – a great blood-red scar had formed over the gaping socket – Silverhair saw her banging her head against rock outcrops, as if trying to shake loose the pain of the tusk root. Snagtooth had a great deal of difficulty sleeping; even the back-and-forth movement of her jaw when eating seemed to hurt her.

And Snagtooth was not one to suffer in silence.

She complained, snapped, and refused to do her fair share of digging, even expecting Silverhair and Eggtusk to find her rich clumps of grass and rip them out and carry them to her ever-open mouth. Silverhair could see why Owlheart had taken the opportunity to send her away from Foxeye and the calves for a while.

'I put up with it because I can see she is suffering,' grumbled Eggtusk to Silverhair. 'Perhaps she has an abscess.'

If so, that was bad news; there was no way to treat such an agonising collection of poison in the mouth, and Snagtooth would simply have to hope it cleared up of its own accord. If it didn't, it could kill her.

Poor Eggtusk, meanwhile, was having his own trouble with warble flies. Silverhair could see maggots dropping out of red-rimmed craters in his skin, heading for the ground to pupate. Unnoticed, the flies must have laid eggs in his fur last summer. The eggs quickly hatched and the maggots burrowed into Eggtusk's tissue, migrating around the body before coming to rest near the skin of his back. Here they would have continued to grow through the winter and spring in a cavity filled with pus and blood, breathing through an air-hole gnawed in the skin. The eruption of the full-grown larvae was a cause of intense irritation to Eggtusk, who, despite his colourful cursing, was helpless to do anything about it.

And meanwhile the season bloomed around them. As the height of the brief summer approached, the tundra exploded with activity, as plants, animals, birds and insects sought to complete the crucial stages of their annual lives in this brief respite from the grip of winter. The flowers of the tundra opened: white mountain avens, yellow poppies, white heather, crimson, yellow, red, white and purple saxifrage, lousewort, pink primulas, even the orange of marigolds. All the flowers had started their cycle of growth as soon as the snow melted. And the birds were everywhere now. Snow buntings caught crane flies to feed their chicks. Skuas hunted the fledglings of turnstones and sanderlings. As she passed a cliff, Silverhair saw barnacle geese fledglings taking their first tentative steps from their parents' nests far above. This meant jumping. The chicks' stubby wings flapped uselessly, and they fell to the bottom of the cliff. Many chicks died from the fall, and others, trapped in scree, were snapped up by the eager jaws of Arctic foxes.

The silence of the winter was long gone. The air was filled with birdsong – larks and plovers, the haunting calls of loons, irritable jaeger cries – and the buzz of insects, the bark and howls of foxes and wolves. All of it was laced with the occasional agonised scream as some predator attained its goal.

It was a furious chorus of mating and death.

Through this flat, teeming landscape, Silverhair and the others walked stolidly on. When they found a rock face where they could shelter, they slept, as the summer sun scraped its way around the horizon, and the sky faded again to its deepest midnight blue.

Once Silverhair woke to find herself staring at a snowy owl, a mother perched on her nest with her brood of peeping chicks.

The mother was a white bundle of feathers, standing out clearly against grey shale. Her mate coursed over the rough vegetation, searching for lemmings to bring to his nest. The owl chicks had been born at intervals of three or four days, and the oldest chick was substantially bigger than the smallest. Silverhair knew that if some disaster occurred and the owls' food supply was threatened, the largest owlet would eat its smallest sibling – and then the next smallest, and the next.

It was brutal. But it was the owls' way of assuring that at least one youngster survived the harshest times. The little tableau, of beauty and cruelty, seemed to summarise the world, this cruel summer, to Silverhair.

The mother owl beat her broad wings slowly, and stared at Silverhair with great sulphur-yellow eyes.

As the endless day wore towards its golden noon, they drew nearer the place where Lop-ear had fallen.

They reached the low ridge near the south coast. Silverhair remembered this place. It was here she had shared Lop-ear's warmth, here they had encountered the Lost with his thunder-stick, and here she had last seen the body of Lop-ear, like a squat, fur-coated boulder.

The body was gone.

But there were Lost here.

Eggtusk led the two Cows behind an eroded outcrop of rock. The mammoths huddled together uncertainly. Eggtusk raised his trunk cautiously over the rock; the hair of his trunk streamed behind his head.

The mammoths had not been seen. The Lost didn't seem very observant; none of them was maintaining a watch for wolves – or mammoths, come to that.

The Lost were sitting in a loose circle on the ground. There were six of them. Three of them carried thunder-sticks, like the one which Skin-of-Ice had used against Lop-ear. And one of them – Silverhair could never forget that smooth, unnatural, hairless head – was Skin-of-Ice himself.

The Lost surrounded the carcass of what looked like a fox. And they were drinking a clear fluid from flasks, which they passed from paw to paw. They sat unnaturally upright, with strange sets of loose skin over their bodies, and only a few patches of fur on their scalps and faces.

They were like wolves, she thought. Predators, working at a downed prey. But then they were *not* like wolves, for they did not work at the fox's body with their teeth and claws as wolves will. Rather, they had ice-claws – as she called them, for they were made of something that gleamed like sea ice – ice-claws that they held in their paws, and used to cut into the fox's passive body.

The Lost were grimy, listless, steeped in misery. They seemed to bicker and snap at each other, sometimes descending into clumsy fights.

All but Skin-of-Ice. He sat apart from the rest, thunder-stick on his lap, watching the others coldly.

Silverhair felt a cold, hard determination gathering inside her. All her naive dreams of finding some opportunity to work with the Lost had evaporated with the blows inflicted on Lop-ear. These are my enemy, she thought. I will not live in a world which contains them, and I will oppose them to my dying breath.

But to do that, I must understand them.

'We're in no danger here,' said Eggtusk in a soft rumble, inaudible to the Lost. 'I'm sure they can't see us. According to the Cycle the Lost have poor hearing and smell, and we're downwind of them. And besides, three grown mammoths against six – or sixty – of those skinny creatures should be no match.'

Silverhair growled: 'They have thunder-sticks.'

'Those spindly things? What harm can they do us?'

Silverhair knew it was difficult for him to imagine, for sticks which spat fire and agony on command had no place in a mammoth's map of the world. 'Eggtusk, a thunder-stick killed Lop-ear. Skin-of-Ice didn't even have to come close to us to do it.'

'Then what should we do?'

'It's obvious,' complained Snagtooth loudly. 'We must creep away from this place of blood and Lost, and—'

Eggtusk slapped his trunk over her head. 'Quiet, you fool.'

Now, to Silverhair's bewilderment, one of the Lost – a fat brute – shucked off layers of his loose outer skin from his body. His hairless chest and forelimbs were pink and gleaming with sweat. He swung his ice-claw down through the air, hauling it with both paws. He cracked the fox's strong leg bones, tore through its skin, cut tendons, prised open ribs and ripped open the organs that had nestled inside the fox's body.

As he worked, the Lost made a noise like the caw of a gull. Almost joyous.

When he was done, this savage one opened the fox's mouth and reached inside. With a fast slash of his ice-claw he severed the fox's tongue. Then he lifted the limp, fleshy thing above his head, cawing and rubbing his big belly, as if this was the finest delicacy.

'They are like worms,' Eggtusk whispered, beside Silverhair. 'They gnaw on the meat of the dead.' Silverhair could hear the anger and disgust in his voice. 'Especially that fat one.'

'Gull-Caw,' Silverhair said.

'What?'

'We will call him Gull-Caw.'

Eggtusk was silent for a few heartbeats. Then he said, 'We must not hate them. They are Hotbloods, like us. And they have their place in the Cycle. Whatever they do. After all, it is not pleasant to watch a pack of wolves work at a seal's carcass—'

Silverhair said, 'Wolves take what they need. Even the worms do no more than that. There is none of this joy in death and the tearing apart of the body. These Lost are *not* like us, Eggtusk.'

He looked at her. 'It was you,' he reminded her, 'who wanted to seek out the Lost. Get help from them.'

'I was wrong,' she said tightly. 'I never imagined how wrong.'

Snagtooth, on Silverhair's other flank, was staring, fascinated. 'Look at the way they work together.'

'You sound as if you admire them,' Eggtusk snapped.

Snagtooth grunted. 'They are small and weak and isolated on this Island, but they are not slowly dying, as we are. They are not like us. Perhaps they are *better*.'

Silverhair, shocked more deeply by Snagtooth than she had thought possible, watched as the Lost completed their grisly butchering.

And she wondered what had become of Lop-ear. Was it possible his helpless body had received the same fate as the fox?

. . . There was a crack, like thunder.

All three mammoths raised their trunks and trumpeted.

Eggtusk had twisted his head and was staring at his shoulder. 'By Kilukpuk's oozing scabs—' Blood was seeping out of a small puncture in his hide, and spreading over his wiry hair.

But Silverhair scarcely noticed this. For, standing only a few strides downwind of them, were two of the Lost: Skin-of-Ice, and Gull-Caw. They were both holding thunder-sticks.

And they smelled of mammoth: for they had smeared themselves in mammoth dung, the rich, dark stuff clinging to their loose outer skin and their bare faces. That was how they had crept up unnoticed.

Even at this moment of peril, Silverhair felt chilled at the cunning of the Lost.

Eggtusk reared on his hind legs, raised his trunk and trumpeted. 'So you'd punch a hole in me, eh?' he roared. 'By Kilukpuk's quivering dugs, we'll see about that.' The great Bull's forefeet crashed back to the earth, and the ground shook as he lowered his head and charged.

The thunder-sticks wavered. Faced by a trumpeting, hurtling mountain of muscle, flesh and tusks, the two Lost ran, scampering across the flower-strewn plain like two Arctic hares.

Suddenly, to Silverhair, they did not seem a threat at all. But, she reminded herself, they still carried their thunder-sticks.

With Snagtooth, she ran after Eggtusk.

Skin-of-Ice fell, heavily, and cried out. When he got to his feet again he was clutching his foreleg.

Gull-Caw came back to him. The two Lost stood side by side and raised their sticks.

More thunder-cracks.

Silverhair felt something fly past her ear, a hot scorch. And another crack, and another: a series of rippling explosions like the splintering of a falling tree, sharp sounds that rolled away across the plain.

Eggtusk grunted and staggered. Silverhair saw a new splash of blood on his fleshy thigh. 'Get behind me,' Eggtusk ordered.

'But—'

'Do as he says,' snapped Snagtooth. Her eyes were wide, her smashed tusk dribbling fresh pulp.

Silverhair tucked herself, with Snagtooth, behind Eggtusk's mighty buttocks.

And now Eggtusk began to walk towards the Lost, his pace measured and deliberate. 'So you think you can kill me, do you, little maggots? We'll see about that. Do you know what I'm going to do with you? I'm going to pick you up with my trunk and drown you in the pus which oozes from Kilukpuk's suppurating mouth-ulcers. And then—'

But still the thunder-sticks barked, and the strange, invisible, deadly insects slammed into Eggtusk's giant body. One of them tore away a piece of his shoulder, and Silverhair's face was splashed by a horrific spray of hair, skin and pulped flesh.

With each impact Eggtusk staggered. But he did not fall, and he kept the Lost washed in a stream of obscene threats.

Gull-Caw was agitated. The fat one's thunder-stick no longer barked; he was scrabbling at it, frightened, frustrated.

When Skin-of-Ice saw this, he turned and ran.

Gull-Caw roared out his anger at this betrayal. Then, seeing Eggtusk remorselessly approaching, he yowled like a fox cub. He dropped his useless thunder-stick and turned to run, but he stumbled and fell on the ground.

And now Eggtusk was over him.

The great Bull reared up, raising his huge tree-trunk legs high in the air. His deformed tusk glistened, dripping with his own blood; he raised his trunk and trumpeted so loud his voice echoed off the icebergs of the distant ocean.

Silverhair reared back, terrified of him herself.

Eggtusk reached down and wrapped his trunk around the wriggling Lost. He lifted the fat body effortlessly. Eggtusk squeezed, the immense muscles of his trunk wrapped tightly around the Lost's greasy torso. Silverhair could see the Lost's eyes bulge, his short pink tongue protrude.

Then Eggtusk threw Gull-Caw into the air. The Lost briefly flew, yelling, his fat limbs writhing, his smooth, ugly skin now smeared with Eggtusk's blood.

The Lost landed heavily on his belly; Silverhair heard the crack of bone.

But still Gull-Caw tried to raise himself, to crawl away, to reach with a bloodied forelimb for his thunder-stick.

Eggtusk leaned forward and knelt on the Lost's back.

The Lost screamed as that great weight bore down. Silverhair heard the crunch of ribs and vertebrae. The Lost's scream turned to a liquid gurgle, and blood gushed from his mouth.

And then Eggtusk drove a tusk through his neck, pinning him to the ground.

The Lost twitched once, twice more. Then he was still.

Chapter Five

THE KETTLE HOLE

Eggtusk pulled his tusk from the body, shaking it to free it of the limp remnant flesh of the Lost. He rooted for the thunder-stick. He curled his trunk-fingers around the black, spindly thing, and lifted it high in the air. 'It feels cold.'

'It's a thing of death,' said Silverhair.

Eggtusk raised the thunder-stick and smashed it against a rock outcrop until it was bent in two, and small parts had come tumbling from it. He hurled the wreckage far into the grass. Then he wiped his tusk against the outcrop, to free it of blood and scraps of flesh.

'Now come,' said Eggtusk. 'We will honour the body of this Lost I have killed.' And he bent down, wincing slightly, and ripped yellow tundra flowers from the ground. He lumbered over to the corpse and sprinkled the flowers there. He was a fearsome sight, with his face masked in blood, one of his eyes concealed by blood-matted hair, and thunder-stick punctures over his legs and chest. Even his trunk had a bite taken out of it.

After a few heartbeats, Silverhair and Snagtooth joined in. Soon the carcass of the Lost was buried in grass and flowers. They stood over the corpse as the sun wheeled through the icy sky, Remembering the fat, ugly creature as best they could.

'Let that be an end of it,' growled Eggtusk. 'Once I destroyed a wolf that had come stalking the Family. We never saw that pack again. The Cycle teaches that mammoths should kill only when we have to. We have frightened the Lost so badly they'll respect us, and never come near us again . . .'

Silverhair wanted to believe that was true. But she was unsure. She had watched the way the Lost had carved slices out of that fox. There had been a *joy* in their behaviour. An evil triumph.

She couldn't help but feel that a world free of Skin-of-Ice would be a better place. And, she feared, the killing wasn't done yet.

Silverhair tried to treat Eggtusk's many wounds. They found a stream, and she bathed him with trunkfuls of cold, clear water, washing away the matted blood and dirt in his fur, and she plastered mud over the worst wounds in his flesh. But the pain of the wounds was very great. And she could see that some of them were becoming infected, despite her best ministrations with mud and leaves.

But Eggtusk was impatient to move on. 'I don't think that other worm will pose any threat to us. He can't have got far. Come on. We'll follow him.'

Silverhair was startled. 'We aren't wolves to track prey, Eggtusk.'

'And he still has the thunder-stick,' Snagtooth said, her voice without expression.

'That Lost was wounded,' Eggtusk said firmly. 'If he's died in some hole, we'll honour him. Maybe, if he's alive, we'll be able to help him.'

That seemed extremely unlikely to Silverhair. And besides, there were the other Lost to think about; what had become of them while the mammoths had chased Gull-Caw? Perhaps Eggtusk's thinking was muddled by pain . . .

But there was no more time to debate the issue; for already Eggtusk was limping off to the south, the direction Skin-of-Ice had fled.

As browsing grass-eaters, mammoths are poor trackers. As the Cycle says, *It doesn't take the skill of a wolf to sneak up on a blade of grass*. Nevertheless, it was surprisingly easy to track the progress the Lost, Skin-of-Ice, had made towards the southern coast.

Eggtusk charged ahead over the plain. 'Here is grass he crushed,' he said. 'Here is a splash of his blood, on this rock. You see? And here is a dribble of urine . . . I can still smell it . . .'

Silverhair and Snagtooth followed, more uncertainly. All Silverhair could smell right now was the stink of Eggtusk's decaying wounds.

'Of course,' said Snagtooth softly to Silverhair, 'it may be that this Lost *wants* us to find him.'

Silverhair was startled. 'But Eggtusk nearly killed him.'

'I know,' said Snagtooth. 'But who knows what goes on in the mind of a Lost?'

Silverhair kept her counsel. Perhaps Eggtusk was launching himself into this quest to take his mind off his wounds. Maybe, when his injuries had healed sufficiently for him to start thinking more clearly, she could persuade him to return to the Family, and then—

Suddenly Eggtusk trumpeted in triumph.

Silverhair slowed and stood beside him.

The Lost, Skin-of-Ice, was lying on the ground, face down, still some distance away. He wasn't moving. There was no sign of his thunder-stick. The ground between the Lost and the mammoths was hummocky, broken, tufted with grass and sprinkled with residual ice scraps.

There was no sound, no scent, and she could see the Lost only indistinctly.

The grey cap of hair on Silverhair's scalp prickled. 'I wish I knew where his thunder-stick is,' she murmured. 'We ought to be careful—'

But Eggtusk was already lumbering ahead, his trunk raised in greeting to the Lost he intended to help.

He approached a patch of ground strewn with grass and broken bushes – even a few spruce branches. Silverhair stared at the patch of ground, wondering what could have made such a mess. Wolves? Birds? But there was no scent; no scent at all.

Suddenly she was alarmed. 'Eggtusk! Take care—'

Eggtusk, his massive feet pounding at the ground, reached the debris-strewn patch.

With a cracking of twigs and branches, the ground opened up beneath his forefeet. He fell into a pit, amid an explosion of shattered branches and clumps of grass.

Silverhair charged forward. 'Eggtusk! Eggtusk!'

She could see the dome of his head and the hair of his broad back, protruding from the hole. And now his trumpeting turned to a roar of anguish.

But Snagtooth was tugging at her tail. 'Keep back! It's a kettle hole . . .'

Silverhair, despite her impatience and fear, knew that

Snagtooth was right. It would help no one if she got trapped herself.

She slowed, and took measured steps towards the hole in the ground, testing each footfall. Soon she was walking over the leaves and twigs and grass which had concealed the hole.

Eggtusk was embedded in the hole, a few blades of muddy grass scattered over his back. His trunk lay on the ground, and his great tusks, stained by mud and blood, protruded uselessly before him. He was out of her reach.

As she approached he tried to lift and turn his head. He said, 'Don't come any closer.'

'Are you stuck?'

Eggtusk growled wearily. 'By Kilukpuk's snot-crusted nostril hair, what a stupid question. Of course I'm stuck. My legs are wedged in under me. I can't even move them.'

A kettle hole was a hazard of their warming times, Silverhair knew. It formed when a large block of ice was left by a retreating glacier. Sediment would settle over the ice, burying it. Then, as the ice melted, the resulting water would seep away and the sinking sediment, turning to mud, would subside to form a sticky hole in the ground.

Deadly, for any mammoth foolish enough to stray into one. But—

'Eggtusk, kettle holes are easy to spot. Only a calf would blunder into one.'

'Thank you for that,' he snorted. 'Don't you see? It's your friend Skin-of-Ice. Snagtooth was right. That wretched worm did want us to follow him. While we honoured his fallen comrade, Skin-of-Ice was preparing this trap for us. And I was fool enough to charge right in . . .'

He subsided. His breath was a rattle, and he seemed to be weakening. He tried to raise his trunk, then let it flop back feebly to the ground.

Silverhair tried to step forward, but her feet sank deeper into the mud that surrounded the hole. She felt an agitated anger; she had seen too much death this blighted summer. 'You aren't going to do this to me,' she cried. 'Not yet, you old fool!'

She scrambled back to firm ground, and forced herself to think.

She threw branches and twigs over the ground and walked forward on them. Spreading the load helped her keep out of the mud for a little further, but in the end her weight was just too great, and each time she tried to get closer to Eggtusk she was forced to back up.

Well, if she couldn't reach Eggtusk, maybe he could get himself out.

She gathered branches and threw them towards Eggtusk's head. If he could pull them into the pit he might be able to use them to get a grip with his feet.

But even when he managed to grab the branches he seemed too weak, too firmly stuck, to do anything with them.

Despairing, she looked for Snagtooth, seeking help. But Snagtooth was gone: there was no trace of her musk on the wind, no echo of her voice.

But, Silverhair admitted, it wasn't important. Snagtooth's mind was almost as impenetrable as a Lost's, and since her injury that had only worsened. She would be no help anyhow.

. . . And Skin-of-Ice, she noticed, was gone too. Perhaps he had crawled away to die at last. Somehow she suspected it would not be so easy. But she had no time, no energy for him now.

Silverhair brought Eggtusk food, grass and twigs and herbs. But the wind scattered the grass, and Eggtusk's trunk-fingers seemed to be losing their co-ordination and were having increasing difficulty in grasping the food.

But she kept trying, over and over.

'Do not fret, little Silverhair,' he said to her, and his voice was a bubbling growl. 'You've done your best.'

'Eggtusk—'

He reached out with his trunk as if to stroke her head, but it was, of course, much too far to reach. 'Give it up. That Lost has trapped me and killed me. I am already dead.'

'No!'

'You have to go back to the Family, tell them what has happened. Owlheart will know what to do . . . Tell her I'm sorry I didn't keep my promise to bring you home. And you must tell Croptail that he is the dominant Bull now. Tell him I'm sorry I won't be there to teach him any more . . . Do it, Silverhair. Go . . .'

'I won't leave you,' she said.

'By Kilukpuk's mould-choked pores, you always were stubborn.'

'And you've always been so strong—'

'Should take more than a little hunger to kill old Eggtusk, eh? But it isn't just that. Watch now.'

With infinite difficulty, he rolled his trunk towards him, and pushed it below his chin and into the pit, below his body. She could see the muscles of his upper trunk spasm, as if he was tugging at something.

Painfully, carefully, he pulled his trunk out of the pit. He was holding something.

It was a bone, she saw. A rib. It was crusted with dried, blackened blood – and stained with a fresher crimson.

A mammoth rib.

'The bottom of the pit is littered with them,' gasped Eggtusk. 'They stick up everywhere. Mostly into me. And I think Skin-of-Ice put some kind of poison on them.'

'They took it from the *yedoma*,' she said. Or – worse still –

from Lop-ear . . . She felt bile rise in her throat. 'They are using our own bones to kill us.'

'Oh, these Lost are clever,' he said. 'Snagtooth was right about that. I couldn't have dreamed how clever.' He let the rib fall to the mud. 'Well, little Silverhair. If you're determined to hang around here, you can help me. There's something I must do while I still have the strength.'

'What?'

'Fetch a rock. As big as you can throw over to me.'

She went to an outcrop of rock and obeyed, bringing back a big sandstone boulder. She stood at the edge of the kettle hole, dug her tusks under the rock and sent it flying through the air towards Eggtusk. It landed before his face, splashing in the mud.

He raised his head, turned it sideways. And he brought his misshapen tusk crashing against the rock. The tusk cracked, but he showed no awareness of the pain.

'Eggtusk! What are you doing?'

'You needn't try to stop me,' he said, breathing hard.

'*Why?*'

'Better I do it than the Lost. Didn't you tell me how they robbed the ancient mammoth in the *yedoma*? I don't want them doing the same to me.'

And again he began to smash his magnificent deformed tusk against the rock, until it had splintered and cracked at the base.

At last it tore loose, leaving only a bloody spike of ivory protruding from the socket in his face.

'Take it,' he told Silverhair, his voice thick with blood. 'You can reach it. Take it and smash it to splinters.'

She was weeping openly now. But she reached out over the mud of the kettle hole, wrapped her trunk around the tusk, and pulled it to her. It was immense: so massive she could barely lift it. Once again she appreciated the huge strength of Eggtusk – strength that was dissipating into the cold mud as she watched.

She lugged the tusk to the outcrop of sandstone, and pounded it until it had splintered and smashed to fragments.

Eggtusk rested for a time. Then he lifted his head again, and started to work on his other tusk.

When he was done, his face was half-buried in the mud, the breath whistling through his trunk; there was blood around his mouth, and pulp leaked from the stumps of his tusks.

'Eggtusk—'

'Little Silverhair. You're still here? You always were stubborn . . . Talk to me.'

'Talk to you?'

'Tell me a story. Tell me about Ganesha.'

And so she did. Gathering her strength, staying the weakening of her own voice, she told him the ancient tale of Ganesha the Wise, and how she had prepared her calf Prima to conquer the cold lands.

He grunted and sighed, seeming to respond to the rhythms of the ancient story.

. . . She woke with a start. She hadn't meant to sleep.

Eggtusk, still wedged tight in his kettle hole, was chewing on something. 'This grass is fine. Isn't it, Wolfnose? The finest I ever tasted. And this water is as clear and fresh as if it had just melted off the glacier.'

But she could see that only blood trickled from his mouth, and all that he chewed was a mouthful of his own hair, ripped from his back.

'Eggtusk—'

He raised his head, and the stumps of his tusks gleamed in the sun. 'Wolfnose? Remember me, Wolfnose. Remember me. I see you. I'm coming now . . .'

And his great head dropped to the earth, and did not rise again.

Silverhair felt the deepest dark of despair settle over her, an anguish of shame and frustration that she hadn't been able to help him.

Soon she must start the Remembering. She could not reach Eggtusk, or touch his body; but at least she could cover his corpse—

Suddenly there was a band of fire around her neck: a band that dug deep into her flesh. She trumpeted her shock and pain.

And the Lost were here, dancing before her, two of them, and they held sticks in their paws, sticks attached to whatever was wrapped around her neck.

Snagtooth was standing before her, apparently in no distress.

Silverhair, shocked, agonised, tried to speak. When the Lost tugged at their sticks the fire in her neck deepened, so tight she could barely breathe. 'Snagtooth . . . help me . . .'

But Snagtooth kept her trunk down. 'I brought them here.'

'You did what?'

'Don't you see? *They are smarter than we are*. Submit to them, Silverhair. It isn't so bad.'

'No—' Silverhair struggled to stay on her feet, to ignore the pain in her throat.

And beyond Snagtooth, she saw Skin-of-Ice himself. His damaged foreleg was strapped to his chest.

Light as a hare, he hopped over the mud of the kettle hole, and came to rest on Eggtusk's broad, unmoving back. He raised his head to the sky and let loose a howl of triumph.

Then he raised an ice-claw in his paw, and drove it deep into Eggtusk's helpless back.

The thing around Silverhair's neck tightened. A red mist filled her vision.

She was forced to her knees.

Chapter Six

THE CAPTIVE

The Lost threw more loops and lassos at her. Many of them missed, or she shook them off easily, but gradually they caught on her tusks or trunk or around her legs. Soon her head was so heavy with ropes that she could not lift it.

Now the Lost – five or six of them, under the supervision of Skin-of-Ice – began to run around her, whooping, and beating at her flanks and legs with sticks. She tried to reach them with her tusks – she knew she could disembowel any of these weak creatures with a flick of her head – but she was pinned, and they were too clever to come close enough to give her the chance to hurt them.

She could not even lift her head to trumpet, and that shamed her more than anything else.

At last Skin-of-Ice himself came forward. His small teeth showed white in his loathsome, naked face as he bent to peer into her eyes. His mouth, a soft, round thing, was flapping and making noises.

She managed to haul herself back a pace or two. But he stood his ground, and the weight dragging at her forced her to submission once more.

Now he raised a stick, about as long as his foreleg, in the tip of which he had embedded one of his gleaming ice-claws. He held it up before her, waving it before her eyes, as if to demonstrate to her what it was.

One of the other Lost came up. He pawed at Skin-of-Ice, as if trying to restrain him. But Skin-of-Ice shook him off.

Then, with brutal suddenness, Skin-of-Ice lashed out.

He slammed the stick against her face, and the claw penetrated her cheek. The pain was liquid fire.

She kept her gaze on Skin-of-Ice, refusing even to flinch as the pain burned into her.

He threw down his goad and reached forward to her cheek. His paw came away smeared with her blood – and it cupped a brimming pool of her tears, tears she could not help but spill.

Skin-of-Ice threw the tears back in her face, so that they stung her eyes.

As the sun sank towards the horizon, the Lost gathered loose branches and twigs into a rough heap. This heap somehow erupted into flame, as if at the command of the Lost. They did not seem to fear the fire. Indeed, they fed it with more branches, which they boldly threw on to the embers, and stayed close to it, rubbing their paws as if dependent on the fire for warmth.

After a time a knot of hunger gathered in Silverhair's stomach, but the Lost would not let her feed. Even when she passed dung, which the Lost could scarcely prevent, they would kick and prod at her so that her stomach clenched, and they picked up the dung and threw it in her face.

Mammoths need a great deal of food daily, and in fact spend much of each day feeding and drinking. To be kept from doing that was a great torment to Silverhair, and she weakened rapidly.

The Lost were not organised in this. They were careless, lethargic, and seemed to spend a lot of their time asleep.

All save Skin-of-Ice. It was Skin-of-Ice who drove on the others, like a lead Bull, making them work when they would rather sleep or feed or squabble, maintaining the slow cruelty inflicted on Silverhair. All the Lost were repulsive. But it was Skin-of-Ice, she saw, who was the source of evil here.

Meanwhile, as the shadows stretched over the tundra, a group of the Lost worked in the pit which had trapped and killed Eggtusk.

Eggtusk was still upright in the pit, his legs trapped out of sight, his head supported by the stumps of his tusks. The blood that had seeped out of his wounds had soaked the ground around the pit, making it black. His body was already rigid with death, and perhaps half-frozen too.

Now the Lost slung ropes around Eggtusk and hauled. At first they could not budge the passive carcass, but they made a rhythmic noise and concerted their efforts.

At last they managed to drag Eggtusk out of the hole.

Silverhair could hear the crackle of frost-ridden fur as Eggtusk was rolled on to his back, exposing his softer underbelly, and then the more ominous crack of snapping bone. His head settled back to the cold earth, and his mouth gaped. Silverhair could see how the dried blood and dirt matted the great wounds in his chest and belly, and his stomach was swollen and hard.

It was Skin-of-Ice himself who began it.

He took an ice-claw and thrust it into Eggtusk's lower belly. Then, bracing himself and using both paws, he dragged the claw up the length of Eggtusk's body, cutting through hair and flesh, in a line from anus to throat. Silverhair felt the incision as if it had been made in her own body.

Then, under the direction of Skin-of-Ice, the Lost reluctantly gathered to either side of Eggtusk. They dug their forelimbs into the new wound in his belly, grabbed his ribcage, and hauled back. The ribcage opened like a grotesque flower, the white of bone emerging from the red-black wound.

Eggtusk was opened up, splayed.

Skin-of-Ice now climbed *inside* the body of Eggtusk. He reached down and, with his forelegs, began to dig out Eggtusk's internal organs: heart, liver, a great rope of intestine.

Another of the Lost turned away, and vomit spilled from his mouth.

When Skin-of-Ice was done, the Lost took hold of Eggtusk's legs and hauled him away from the steaming pile of guts they had removed from the carcass. Then they turned Eggtusk over again; this time he slumped, almost shapeless, against the ground.

The Lost began to hack at the skin of Eggtusk's legs and around his neck. When it was cut through, they dug their small forelimbs inside the skin and began to haul it off the sheets of muscle and fat that coated Eggtusk's body. It came loose with a moist rip. Wherever it stuck, Skin-of-Ice or one of the others would hack at the muscle inside the skin, or else reach underneath and punch at the skin from the inside.

At last, the skin had come free from Eggtusk's back, belly and neck, a great sheet of it, bloody on the underside and dangling clumps of hair on the other. Silverhair could see it was punctured by the many wounds he had suffered.

The Lost folded up the skin and put it to one side. Eggtusk's flayed carcass was left as a mass of exposed muscle and flesh.

Now the Lost took their ice claws and began to hack in earnest at the carcass. They seemed to be trying to sever the flesh from Eggtusk's legs, belly and neck in great sections. They even cut away his tail, ears and part of his trunk.

When they were done, Eggtusk's body had been comprehensively destroyed.

But now there came a still worse horror; for the Lost began to throw lumps of dripping flesh on the fire – Eggtusk's flesh – and, when it was all but burned, they dragged it off the fire, sliced it into pieces and crammed it into their small mouths, with every expression of relish.

Silverhair forced herself to watch, to witness every cut and savour every fresh stink, and remember it all.

The Lost seemed baffled by the absence of the old Bull's tusks, and they spent some time inspecting the bloody stumps in his face. Silverhair realised that Eggtusk had been right. For some reason the loathsome souls of these Lost cherished the theft of tusks above all, and even as he lay trapped and dying Eggtusk had defied his killers.

She clutched that to her heart, and tried to draw courage from Eggtusk's example.

But there was little time for such reflection, for the goading she endured continued, without relief. Soon her need for sleep drove all other thoughts from her mind, and the ache from the injuries to her neck and cheek refused to subside.

Snagtooth was not mistreated as Silverhair was. She was bound by a single loop of rope fixed to a stake driven into the ground. Silverhair thought that with a single yank Snagtooth could surely drag the stake out of the ground. But she seemed to have no such intention.

Skin-of-Ice came to Snagtooth, so close she could have gutted him with a single flick of her remaining tusk. But Snagtooth dipped her head and let the Lost touch her. He brought her food: pawfuls of grass which he lifted up to her, and water in a shell-like container which he carried from a stream. Passively Snagtooth dipped her trunk into the shell thing. She even lifted her trunk, and Silverhair watched her tongue slick out, pink and moist, to accept the grass from the paw of her captor.

With the watery sun once more climbing the sky, Silverhair saw, in her bleary vision, that Skin-of-Ice had come to stand before her.

He reached towards her with one paw, as if making to stroke her as he had Snagtooth. But Silverhair rumbled and pulled her head away from him.

Before she had time even to see its approach, his goad had slapped at her cheek. She could feel the scabs which had crusted over her earlier wounds break open once more, and the pain was so intense she could not help but cry out.

Now Skin-of-Ice turned to his companions and gestured with his goad.

Immediately the pressure around her throat and across her back intensified. She was forced to kneel in the dirt. Under her belly hair, she could feel the stale warmth of her own dung.

And now Skin-of-Ice stepped forward. She could feel him grab her hair, step on one prone leg, and hoist himself up on to her back so that he was sitting astride her. The Lost around her were cawing and slapping their paws together, in evident approval of Skin-of-Ice's antics.

She strained her muscles and tried to dislodge him, but she could not stand, let alone rear; she could not remove this maddening, tormenting worm from her back.

Now the pressure of the ropes lessened, and the Lost came forward and began to prod at her belly. Reluctant though she was to do anything in response to their vicious commands, she clambered slowly to her feet. As she did so, she could feel how

Skin-of-Ice wrapped his paws in her long hair to keep from falling off.

The Lost moved around behind her, and she could feel a new load being added to her back: something unmoving which had to be tied in place with ropes around her belly.

She could not see what this load was. But she could smell it. It was the remnants of Eggtusk: bones, skin and dismembered meat. She tried to shake the load loose, but the ropes were too tight.

The Lost moved around her belly, loosening the ropes which bound up her legs. Skin-of-Ice pulled her ears and slapped at her with his own goad. The Lost before her were dragging at the ropes around her head and trunk.

What they intended was obvious. They wanted her to walk with them to their nest at the south of the Island, to carry the dishonoured, mutilated corpse for them.

But she stood firm. She could not escape, but, even as weak as she was, the Lost were not strong enough to haul her against her will.

Now a new rope was attached to her neck. A pair of Lost pulled it across the tundra, and attached it to the collar around Snagtooth's neck.

And Snagtooth – led by her trunk, held in the paw of one of the Lost, but otherwise under no duress or goad – began to walk, deliberately, to the south. The rope between the two mammoths stretched taut, and began to drag at Silverhair's neck. And the monster on her back lashed at her with his goad.

Silverhair's feet slipped on the dusty ground. She took one step, then another. She could resist the feeble muscles of any number of the Lost, but, weak and starved as she was, not the hauling of an adult mammoth.

She tried to call to Snagtooth: 'Why are you doing this? How can you help them?'

But her voice was weak and muffled. Snagtooth did not hear, or perhaps chose not to; she kept her face firmly turned to the south.

And, as she stumbled forward from step to step, constantly impeded by the ropes which still looped between her legs, Silverhair felt her shame was complete.

They reached the coast, not far from the place where Silverhair had first encountered Skin-of-Ice.

Silverhair was hauled along the beach.

She saw, groggily, that the season was well advanced. The sea was full of noise and motion. The remnant ice was breaking up quickly now, with bangs and cracks. Small icebergs were swept past in the current. She saw a berg strike pack ice ahead and rear up out of the water, before falling back with a ponderous splash.

She was led past a floe where a large male polar bear lay silently beside a seal's breathing hole. With startling suddenness the bear dived into the pool, and, after much thrashing, emerged with its jaws clamped around the neck of a huge ringed seal. The incautious seal was dragged through a breathing hole no wider than its head, and there was soft crunching as the bones of the seal's body were broken or dislocated against the ice. Then, with a cuff of its mighty paw, the bear slit open the seal and began to strip the rich blubber from the inside of its skin.

It seemed to Silverhair that the seal was still alive.

Silverhair was dragged away from the bear and its victim. Even the Lost, she realised, were wise enough to watch the bear with caution.

At the top of the beach, away from the reach of the tide, the Lost had made their nest.

There were more Lost here. They moved forward, hesitantly, but with curiosity. They approached Snagtooth, and she allowed them to touch her trunk and tug at the fur of her belly. Even when one of them prodded at the stump of her broken tusk, an action that must have been agonisingly painful, she did little more than flinch.

Even on first contact with the mammoths, the Lost seemed to have no fear, so secure were they in their dominance of the world around them.

Now Silverhair was dragged forward.

The beach was scarred by the blackened remains of fires. She recognised a stack of thunder-sticks, looking no more dangerous than fallen branches. There were little shelters, like caves. They were made of sheets of reddish-brown shiny stuff which appeared to have come from the monstrous hulk she had observed on the shore with Lop-ear, in a time that seemed a Great-Year remote.

There was much she did not understand. There were the straight-edged, hollowed-out boxes from which the Lost extracted their strange, odourless foods. There were the glinting, shining flasks – almost like hollowed-out icicles – from which the Lost would pour a clear liquid down their skinny throats, a liquid over which they fought, which they prized above everything else. There was the box which emitted a deafening, incessant noise, and the other box which glittered with star-like lights, into which one or other of the Lost would bark incessantly.

And all of this strange, horrific place was suffused with the smell of mammoth: dead, decaying, burned mammoth.

The Lost set up four stakes in the ground. They beat them in place with blocks of wood they held in their paws.

Silverhair was led towards the stakes.

One of the Lost walked around her on his skinny hind legs,

plucked at the ropes which bound her grisly load to her belly, and stepped in front of her face to inspect her tusks—

And, stretching her ropes to the limit, she twisted her head and swiped at him. She caught him a glancing blow with the side of her tusk – he was so light and frail she could barely feel the impact – and he sprawled on the ground before her. He howled and squirmed. She raised her foreleg. In an instant she would crush the ribcage of this mewling creature.

But Skin-of-Ice was here. He grabbed the paw of the one on the ground and dragged him away from her.

Now the Lost closed rapidly around her. Commanded by Skin-of-Ice, they prodded, poked and dragged at Silverhair until the four stakes were all around her. Then they tied rope around her legs, so tightly it bit into her flesh, pinning each of her legs to a stake, and she could not move.

Chapter Seven

THE NEST OF THE LOST

The endless day wore on.

Silverhair could not lie down, not even move. And she wasn't allowed to sleep. The Lost tormented her continually.

The stake ropes were never released. Though she chafed against them, she only rubbed raw her own flesh; she could feel how the ropes cut to the very bone of her forelegs.

The Lost would give her no water. Soon it felt as if her trunk was shrivelling like drying grass, and her chest and belly were dry as the bones which had emerged from the *yedoma.*

And they tormented her with food. One of them would hold up succulent grass before her, push it towards her mouth, perhaps even allow a blade or two to touch her tongue. But then, invariably, he would snatch the grass away.

Even when there were no Lost with her – when they were all asleep in their artificial caves, the flasks and scraps of half-chewed mammoth meat scattered around their snoring forms – they would set up one of their deafening noise-making boxes beside her, and its unending stomping ensured she could never sleep.

Snagtooth was kept tied up, in full view of Silverhair. But her tether was just a single rope, her feet were not bound so she was free to move as far as the rope would allow her, and she was fed with pawfuls of grass and containers of water.

Several times a day, Skin-of-Ice or one of the others would climb on the back of Snagtooth. The Lost would kick at the back of her ears, as if trying to drive her forward or back. Snagtooth was rewarded with mouthfuls of food if she guessed what they wanted correctly, and strikes of a goad – not as severely as they beat Silverhair – if she got it wrong. All this was greeted with hoots of laughter from the staggering, swaying Lost.

Silverhair tried to recall the Cycle, the legends of Kilukpuk and Ganesha and Longtusk; but the Cycle seemed a remote irrelevance in this place of horror. At last Silverhair's spirit seemed as if it was half-detached from her body, and even the pain of her poisoned wounds receded from her awareness.

When she was left alone, she would look beyond the camp, seeking solace. Somehow it seemed strange that the world was continuing its ancient cycles, regardless of her own suffering, and the cruel designs of the Lost. But life was carrying on.

The cliffs above this beach were crowded with thousands of eider, kittiwakes, murres and fulmars. Every ledge and crevice was packed with nesting birds, and their noise and smell was overwhelming; so many birds circled in the air they darkened the sky. At the base of the cliffs was a bright carpet of lichens and purple saxifrage, fertilised by the guano from the birds.

Silverhair saw a thick-billed murre taking its turn to sit on its single egg, freeing its partner to seek food at the ice-edge. But when the attention of the murre was distracted, a gull swooped down and easily snatched the egg, swallowing it in a single movement. The distress of the murre pair was obvious, for there might not be time in this short season to raise another egg. Silverhair, despite her own plight, felt a stab of sadness at the small tragedy.

. . . But then Skin-of-Ice would return, sometimes with a flask of liquid in his paw. He would adjust the ropes that pinned her, perhaps tightening them around some already chafed and painful spot. And then he would devise some new way to hurt her.

Some of the Lost seemed to show regret for the suffering they caused. They would hurry past the place she was staked, with their faces averted. Or else they would stand before her and stare at her, their spindly forelegs dangling, their small mouths gaping open; sometimes they would even reach up to her hesitantly, as if to stroke her or feed her.

But not Skin-of-Ice.

He knows I'm conscious, she thought. He knows I'm in here.

He knows what he does hurts me. That's why he does it. The others may kill us for food or skin or bones, but not this one. He enjoys inflicting pain. And he enjoys humiliating.

It was a deliberate cruelty of a type she had never encountered before. And she knew it would not stop until she bent her head to him, as had Snagtooth.

Or until one of them was dead.

'. . . Silverhair. Silverhair. Can you hear me?'

Snagtooth was a silhouette against the dying light of the fire.

'Leave me alone,' said Silverhair.

'You don't understand.' Snagtooth was using the contact rumble, a note so deep it was not muffled by the clatter of the noise-maker beside Silverhair, so deep it would not disturb the light slumbers of the Lost. But her voice sounded oddly distorted, as if she spoke with a trunk full of water.

'What is there to understand? You have given yourself to the Lost.'

'We can't fight them, Silverhair. Think about what the Cycle says. Once the mammoths dominated the north of the whole world. But then the Lost came and took it from us – all of it, except the Island. We have to live as they want us to live. We have no choice.'

'There is always a choice,' rumbled Silverhair.

'I think they want us to work for them. Lifting things, moving things about, in the odd way they have of wanting to reorder everything. But it isn't so bad. When one of them climbs on your back, you don't even feel his weight after a while—'

'You do,' said Silverhair softly. 'Oh, you do.'

'They are feeding me well, Silverhair. They cleaned out my abscess. It doesn't hurt any more. Can you imagine how that *feels*?'

'Is that why you are prepared to bend before them? Because they cleaned out your tusk?'

The rumble fell silent for a long time. Then Snagtooth said, 'Silverhair, I think I understand them. I think I am like them.'

'*Like* the Lost?'

'Look around you. There are no bitches here. No cubs. These Lost are alone. Like a bachelor herd, cut off from the Families. No wonder they are so cruel and unhappy . . . Silverhair, I envy you. I can smell it from here, even above the blood and the rot of your wounds and the burning of Eggtusk's flesh—'

'Smell what?'

'The calf growing inside you.'

Silverhair, startled, listened to the slow oceanic pulsing of her own blood. *Could it be true?*

Snagtooth murmured, 'For me it's different, Silverhair. Year after year my body has absorbed the eggs of my unborn calves, even before they fully form.'

Now, in the midst of her own confusing pulse of joy, Silverhair understood. She should have known: for the Cycle teaches that sterile Cows, unable to produce calves, will sometimes grow as huge as mature Bulls, as if their bodies are seeking to make up in stature what they lack in fertility.

Snagtooth said, 'Now do you understand why I submit to the Lost? Because there is nothing else for me, Silverhair. Nothing.'

And Snagtooth turned her head, and Silverhair saw her clearly for the first time since they had arrived in this nest. 'Oh, Snagtooth . . .'

Snagtooth's trunk was *gone* – her trunk with its hundred thousand muscles, infinitely supple, immensely strong, the trunk which fed her and assuaged her thirst, the trunk which defined her identity as mammoth. Now, in the centre of her face, there was only a bloody stump, grotesquely shadowed by the fire's flickering light.

Snagtooth had allowed the Lost to sever her trunk at its root. She couldn't even feed herself or obtain water; she had made herself completely reliant on the mercy of the Lost, for whatever remained of her life.

The pain must have been blinding.

'It isn't so bad!' Snagtooth wailed thickly. 'Not so bad . . .'

The eternal Arctic day wore on.

Silverhair's stomach was so empty now, her dung so thin, she seemed to have gone beyond the pain of hunger and thirst. She couldn't even pass urine any more. The rope burns on her legs seemed to be rotting, so foul was the stench that came from them. She was giddy from lack of sleep, so much so that sometimes the pain fell away from her and she seemed to be floating, looking down on the fouled, bloody body trapped between the stakes on the ground, flying like a gull halfway to the Sky Steppe.

She tried to sense the new life budding inside her – did it have limbs yet? did it have a trunk? – but she could sense only its glowing, heavy warmth.

At last, one dark and cloudy midnight, the situation came to a head.

Skin-of-Ice approached her. She saw that he was staggering slightly. His hairless head was slick and shining with sweat. In his paw he held a glittering flask, already half empty. He raised it in his paw, almost as a mammoth would raise a trunkful of water. But he drank clumsily, as a mammoth never would, and the fluid spilled over his chin and neck.

She had no idea what the clear fluid was. It certainly wasn't water, for its smell was thin and sharp, like mould. Surely it would only serve to rot him from within. But perhaps that explained why, when the Lost forced this liquid down their throats, they would dance, shout, fight, fall into an uncomfortable sleep far from their nests near the fires or in the artificial caves. Sometimes – she could tell from the stink – they even fouled themselves.

And it was when the clear liquid was inside him that Skin-of-Ice would cause Silverhair the most pain.

He wiped away the mess on his face with his paw. He stalked before her, eyeing her, calculating. Then he turned and barked at the other Lost. Two of them emerged from one of their improvised caves, reluctant, staggering a little. They yapped at Skin-of-Ice, as if protesting. But Skin-of-Ice began to yell at them once more, pointing to the bindings on Silverhair's legs, and then pointing behind him.

Silverhair stood stolidly in her trap. It was obvious she was to face some new horror. Whatever it was, she swore to herself, though she could not mask her weakness, she would show no fear.

The Lost, reluctantly obeying Skin-of-Ice, clustered around the stakes which trapped Silverhair's legs and pulled away the ropes. Her wounds, with their encrusted blood and scab tissue, and half-healed flesh, were ripped open.

Released, her right foreleg crumpled and she dropped to one knee. The blood that flowed in her knees and hips, joints which had been held stiff and unmoving for so long, felt like fire.

But, for the first time since being brought here, Silverhair's legs were free. She stood straight with a great effort.

Now the Lost started to prod at her, and to pull at her ropes. She tried to resist, but she was so weakened now the feeble muscles of these Lost were sufficient to make her walk.

She moved one leg forward, then another. The pain in her hips and shoulders had a stabbing intensity.

But the pain began to ease.

Silverhair had always been blessed by good health, and her constitution was tough – designed, after all, to survive without shelter the rigours of an Arctic winter. Even now she could feel the first inklings of a recovery which might come quickly – if she were ever given the chance.

Her strength was returning. But she did not let her limp become less pronounced. Nor did she raise her head, or fight against the ropes. It occurred to her it might be useful if the Lost did not know how strong she was.

But still, it *hurt*.

As they passed a fire, Skin-of-Ice pulled out burning branches. He kept one himself and passed the others to his companions. Soon the patch of littered beach was illuminated by overlapping, shifting circles of blood-red light, vivid in the subdued midnight glow.

They led her past Snagtooth. Her aunt was still tied loosely by the rope dangling from her neck. The stump of her severed trunk was ugly, but it seemed to be healing over.

Snagtooth turned away.

Silverhair walked on, flanked by the Lost, led by the capering gait of Skin-of-Ice in the flickering light of the torches.

They were dragging her to another shelter: a dome shape a little bigger than the rest. The shelter stank of mammoth. She felt her dry trunk curl.

The other Lost backed away, leaving her with Skin-of-Ice. Almost trustingly, he reached up and grabbed one of the ropes that was attached to the tight noose around her neck. Feigning weakness, she allowed herself to be led forward towards the shelter.

Skin-of-Ice shielded his torch and led her through the shelter's entrance. It was so narrow her flanks brushed its sides.

She felt something soft there. *It felt like hair*: like a mammoth's winter coat.

Inside the shelter was utter darkness, relieved only slightly by a disc of indigo sky that showed through a rent in the roof. The stench of death was almost overpowering.

She wondered dully what the Lost was planning. Perhaps this was the place where Skin-of-Ice would, at last, kill her.

He bent and flicked his torch over a small pile in the middle of the floor. It looked like twigs and branches. A fire started. At first smoke billowed up, and there was a stink of fat. But then the smoke cleared, and the fire burned with a clear, steady light.

She saw that the fire was built from bone shards, smashed and broken. Mammoth bones.

The fire's light grew.

The walls of this shelter were made of some kind of skin.

And the walls' supports were curved, and they gleamed, white as snow.

The supports were mammoth tusks.

The tusks had been driven into the ground, so that their tips met at the apex of the shelter. They were joined at the top by a sleeve of what looked like more bone, to make a continuous arch.

And the wall skins, too, had been taken from mammoths, she saw now: flayed from corpses, scraped and cleaned, rust-brown hair still dangling from them. As she looked down, she saw more bones – jaws and shoulder blades and leg bones as thick as tree-trunks – driven into the ground to fix the skins in place there.

Black dread settled on her as she understood. *This shelter was made entirely from mammoth hide and bone.* It was like being inside an opened-out corpse.

But the horror was not yet done. Skin-of-Ice was pointing at the ground with his paw.

Resting by the doorway was the massive skull of a mammoth. She recognised it. She was looking into the empty eye-sockets of Eggtusk.

Skin-of-Ice was confronting her, his paws spread wide, and he was cawing. She knew that he had brought her here, shown her this final horror, to complete his victory over her.

She began to speak to him. 'Skin-of-Ice, it is you who is defeated,' she said softly. 'For I will not forget what you have done here. And when I put you in the ground, the worms will crawl through your skull and inhabit your emptied chest, as you inhabit these desecrated remains.'

For a heartbeat he seemed taken aback – almost as if he understood that she was speaking to him.

Then he raised his goad.

She summoned all her strength, and reared up. The ropes around her neck and forelegs parted.

Skin-of-Ice, evidently realising his carelessness, fell backwards and sprawled before her.

At last her trunk was free. She raised it and trumpeted. She took a deliberate step towards him.

Even now he showed no fear. He raised a paw and curled it: beckoning her, daring her to approach him.

She stabbed at him with her tusk.

But he was fast. He squirmed sideways.

Her tusk drove into the earth. It hit rock buried there, and she felt its tip splinter and crack.

Skin-of-Ice wriggled away. But a splash of bright fresh red disfigured his side, soaking through the loose skins he wore.

She felt a stab of exultation. She had wounded him.

He scrambled out of the shelter.

She set about wrecking this cave of skin. She trampled on the heap of burning bones. She smashed away the supports which held up the grisly roof. When the layers of flayed skin fell over her, exposing the midnight sky, she shook them away.

All this took mere heartbeats.

Then, with her trunk, she picked up the fragments of skin, and laid them reverently over her back. She found herself breathing hard, her limited reserves of energy already depleted.

She turned to meet her fate.

Beyond the ruins of the hut there was a ring of light: a dozen burning branches held aloft by the paws of the Lost. Several of them had thunder-sticks, which they were pointing towards her. She could see their small eyes, sighting along the sticks at her head and belly.

And there was Skin-of-Ice. He was holding his side, but she could see the blood leaking through his fingers.

She tried to calculate. If she charged directly at him, even if the stinging hail from the thunder-sticks caught her, her sheer momentum could not be stopped. And Skin-of-Ice, wounded as he was, would not be able to evade her this time.

She rumbled to her calf. 'So it is over,' she said. 'But the pain will be mine, not yours. You will not see this terrible world of suffering, dominated by these monsters, these Lost. It will be brief, and then we will be together, in the aurora that burns in the sky . . .'

She lowered her head—

There was a braying, liquid roar.

The Lost scattered and ran, yelling.

A shape loomed out of the shadows: bristling with fur, one tusk held high. It was Snagtooth. Silverhair could see how she trailed the broken length of rope which had restrained her.

Without her trunk Snagtooth was unable to trumpet, but she could roar; and now she roared again. She selected one of the Lost and hurled herself straight towards him. The Lost screamed and raised his thunder-stick. It spat fire, and Silverhair could see how blood splashed over Snagtooth's upper thigh. But the wound did not impede her charge.

Snagtooth's mutilated head rammed directly into the belly of the Lost.

Silverhair heard a single bloody gurgle, the crackle of crushed bone. The Lost was hurled into the air and landed far from the circle of torches.

But this victory was transient. The Lost gathered their courage and turned on Snagtooth. Soon the still air was rent by the noise of thunder-sticks.

Snagtooth reeled. She fell to her knees.

Silverhair screamed: 'Snagtooth!'

Through the storm of noise, Silverhair could hear Snagtooth's rumble. 'Remember me . . .'

And Silverhair understood. In the end, Snagtooth had thrown off her shame. She had chosen to give her life for Silverhair and her calf. Now it was up to Silverhair to get away, to accept that ultimate gift.

She turned away from the noise, the Lost, the agonised shape of Snagtooth, and slipped away into the silvery Arctic light.

The Lost closed around Snagtooth with their thunder-sticks and ice-claws.

THREE

MATRIARCH

THE STORY OF GANESHA THE WISE

This (said Silverhair) is the story of Ganesha, who is called the Wise.

I am talking of a time many Great-Years ago – ten, twelve, perhaps more. In those days, the world was quite different, for it was warmer, and much of the land was covered in a rich Forest.

Now, in such a world you or I would be too hot, and there would be little for us to eat. But Ganesha's Family thought themselves blessed.

For Ganesha's Family, and their Clan and Kin, had lived for a hundred Great-Years in a world awash with heat, and Ganesha had no need to keep herself warm, as you do. And she ate the rich food of the Forest: grass, moss, fruit, even leaves and bark.

If Ganesha was standing before you now you would think her strange indeed.

Though she had a trunk and tusks, she had little fur; her grey skin was exposed to the cooling air, all year round. She had little fat on her lean body, and her ears were large, like huge flapping leaves. And Ganesha was tall – she would have towered over you, little Icebones!

Ganesha had two calves, both Cows, called Prima and Meridi.

Everyone agreed that Meridi was the beauty of the Family: tall, strong, lean, her skin like weathered rock, her trunk as supple as a willow branch. By comparison Prima seemed short and fat and clumsy, her ears and trunk stubby. But Ganesha, of course, loved them both equally, as mothers do.

Now, Ganesha was not called Wise for nothing. She knew the world was changing.

She walked north, to the edge of the Forest, where the trees thinned out, and she looked out over the plains: grassy, endless, stretching to the End of the World. When she was a calf, she remembered clearly, such a walk would have taken many more days.

And if Ganesha stepped out of the Forest, enduring the burning sun of that time, she could see where the Forest had once been. For the land here was littered with fallen, rotten trunks and the remnants of roots, within which insects burrowed.

And Ganesha could smell the ice on the wind, see the scudding of clouds across the sky.

The Cycle teaches us of the great Changes that sweep over the world – Changes that come, not in a year or two or ten, not even in the span of a mammoth's lifetime, but with the passing of the Great-Years.

And that is how Ganesha knew about the great Cold that was sweeping down from out of the north, and how she knew that the Forest was shrinking back to the south, just as the tide recedes from the shore.

Ganesha was concerned for her Family.

She consulted the Cycle – which, even in those days, was

already ancient and rich – but she found no lesson to help her there.

However Ganesha was Wise. As she looked into the vast emptiness that was opening up in the north, Ganesha understood that a great opportunity awaited her calves.

But to take that opportunity she would have to step beyond the Cycle.

Ganesha called her calves to her.

'The Forest is dying,' she said.

Prima, squat and solid, said, 'But the Forest sustains us. What must we do?'

Meridi, tall and beautiful, scoffed at her mother. 'All you have seen is a few dead trees. You are an old fool!'

Ganesha bore this disrespect with tolerance.

'This is what we must do,' she said. 'As the Forest dies back, a new land is revealed. There are no trees, but there are grasses and bushes and other things to eat. And it stretches beyond the horizon – all the way to the End of the World.

'This land is called a Tundra. And, because it is new, the Tundra is empty. You will learn to live on the Tundra, to endure the coming Cold.

'It will not be easy,' she said to them. 'You are creatures of the Forest; to become creatures of the Tundra will be arduous and painful. But if you endure this pain your calves, and their calves, will in time cover the Tundra with great Clans, greater than any the world has seen.'

Prima lowered her trunk soberly. 'Matriarch,' she said, 'show me what to do.'

But Meridi scoffed once more. 'You are an old fool, Ganesha. None of this is in the Cycle. Soon I will be Matriarch, and there will be none of this talk of the Tundra!' And she refused to have anything to do with Ganesha's instruction.

Ganesha was saddened by this, but she said nothing.

Now (said Silverhair), to ready Prima for the Tundra took Ganesha three summers.

In the first summer, she changed Prima's skin. She bit away at Prima's great ears, reducing them to small, round flaps of skin. And she nibbled at Prima's tail, making it shorter and stubbier than her sister's, and she tugged at the skin above Prima's backside so that a flap came down over her anus.

Prima endured the pain of all this with strong silence, for she accepted her mother's wisdom. All these changes would help her skin trap the heat of her body. And so they were good.

But Meridi mocked her sister. 'You are already ugly, little Prima. Now you let Ganesha make you more so!' And Meridi tugged at Prima's distorted ears making them bleed once more.

In the second year, Ganesha made Prima fat. She gathered the richest and most luscious leaves and grass in the Forest, and crammed them into Prima's mouth.

Prima endured this. She understood that to withstand the cold a mammoth must be as round as a boulder, with as much of her body tucked on the inside as possible, and swathed in a great layer of warming fat. And so these changes were also good.

But beautiful Meridi mocked her sister's growing fatness. 'You are already ugly, little Prima, and now with your great belly and your tiny head you are as round as a pebble. Look how tall and lean I am!'

And in the third year Ganesha took Prima to a pit in the ground, left by a rotting tree stump. She bade Prima lie in the pit, then covered her with twigs and blades of grass, and caked the whole of her body with mud and stones. There Prima remained for the whole summer, with only her trunk and mouth and eyes protruding; and Ganesha brought her water and food every day.

And as the mud baked in the sun, the twigs and grasses turned into a thick layer of orange-brown fur, which Prima knew would keep her warm through the long Tundra nights. And so these changes were also good.

But again Meridi mocked her sister. 'You are fat and short, little Prima, and now you are covered with the ugliest fur I have ever seen. Look at my rock-smooth skin, and weep!'

All of this Prima endured.

At the end of the third summer Ganesha presented her two daughters to the Family.

She said: 'I will not serve as your Matriarch any longer, for I am tired and my teeth grow soft. Now, if you wish, you can choose to stay with Meridi, who will lead you deeper into the Forest. Or you can join Prima, and learn to live on the Tundra, as she has. Neither course is easy. But I have taught you that the art of travelling is to pick the least dangerous path.'

And she had Prima and Meridi stand before the assembled Family.

There was Meridi, tall and bare and lean and beautiful, promising the mammoths that if they followed her – and the teachings of the Cycle – they would enjoy rich foliage and deep-green shade, just as they had always known. And there was Prima, a squat, fat, round bundle of brown fur, who promised only hardship, and whose life would not follow the Cycle.

It will not surprise you that most of the Family chose to stay with beautiful Meridi and the Cycle.

But a few chose Prima, and the future.

So the sisters parted. They never saw each other again.

Soon the trees were dying, just as Ganesha had foreseen. Meridi and her folk were forced to venture further and further south.

At last Meridi came to a place where Cousins lived already.

They were Calves of Probos like us, but they had chosen to live in the lush warm south many Great-Years ago. They called themselves *elephants*. And, though the elephants recall the Oath of Kilukpuk, they would not allow Meridi and her mammoths to share their Forest.

All of Meridi's renowned beauty made absolutely no difference.

As the Cold settled on the Earth and the Forest died away, Meridi and her Family dwindled.

Meridi died, hungry and cold and without calves.

And now not one of her beautiful kind is left on the Earth.

Meanwhile Prima took her handful of followers out on to the Tundra. It was hard and cold, but they learned to savour the subtle flavours of the Tundra grasses, and Prima helped them become as she was – as we are now.

And her calves, and her calves' calves, roamed over the northern half of our planet.

Ganesha, you see (concluded Silverhair), was not like other Matriarchs.

Some say Ganesha was a dark figure – perhaps with something of the Lost about her – for she defied the Cycle itself. Well, if that is so, it was a fusion that brought courage and wisdom.

For Ganesha found a way for her daughter Prima to change, to become fit for the new, cold world which was emerging from inside its mask of Forest. None of this was in the Cycle before Ganesha. But she was not afraid to look beyond the Cycle if it did not help her.

And now the story of Ganesha is itself part of the Cycle, and always will be, so she can teach us with her wisdom.

Thus, through paradox, the Cycle renews itself . . .

No, Icebones (said Silverhair), the story isn't done yet. I will tell you what became of Ganesha herself!

Of course she could not follow Prima, for Ganesha had grown up in the Forest, like her mother before her, and her mother before that, in a great line spanning many hundreds of Great-Years.

And so – when the Cold came, and the Forest dwindled – Ganesha sank to her knees, and died, and her Family mourned for many days.

But as long as the Cycle is told, Ganesha will be remembered.

Chapter One

THE HUDDLE

Silverhair heard the ugly cawing of the Lost.

She turned and looked back along the beach. She could see sparks of red light breaking away from the dim glow of the camp. Evidently they had done with Snagtooth, and were pursuing her once more.

She staggered along the beach. But her hind legs were still tightly bound up, and she moved with a clumsy shuffle. The stolen mammoth skin lay on her back; she could feel it, heavy as guilt.

By the low sunlight she could see the pack ice which still lingered in the Channel, ghostly blue. She could smell the sharp salt brine of the sea, and the lapping of the water on the shingle was a soothing, regular sound, so different from the days of clamour she had endured. But the cliff alongside her was steep and obviously impenetrable, even had she been fully fit.

She came to a place where the cliff face had crumbled and fallen in great cracked slabs. Perhaps a stream had once run here.

She turned and began to climb up the rough valley, away from the beach.

It was difficult, for the big stones were slippery with kelp fronds. The ropes which bound her hind legs snagged and caught at the rocks.

. . . Something exploded out of the sky.

She trumpeted in alarm. She heard a flapping like giant wings – but wings that beat faster than any bird's. And there was light, a pool of illumination that hurtled the length of the beach.

Silverhair cowered. Air gushed over her, as if from some tamed windstorm, washing over her face and back; the air stank like a tar pit.

The source of the beam was a thing of straight lines and transparent bubbles, with great wings that whirled above it. It was a huge bird, of light and noise.

The Lost had forgotten Silverhair. They went running towards the light-bird, waving their paws.

Carefully, still hobbled by the ropes on her hind legs, Silverhair limped away towards the heart of the Island.

She found a stream, trickling between an outcrop of broken, worn rocks. The first suck of water was so cold and sharp it sent lances of pain along her dry, inflamed nostrils. She raised her trunk to her mouth. She coughed, explosively; her dry throat expelled every drop of the water. When the coughing fit was done, she tried again. The water seemed to burn her throat as it coursed towards her stomach, but she swallowed hard, refusing to allow her body to reject this bounty.

She used her tusks to get the ropes off her hind legs, and then bathed her wounds. The rope burns had indeed turned brown and grey with poison. She washed them clean and caked them with the thin mud she managed to scrape from the bed of the stream.

She cast about for grass. She found it difficult to grasp the tussocks that grew sparsely here, so stiff had her abused trunk become. The grass felt dry, and her tongue, swollen and sore, could detect no flavour.

Another dry, racking cough, and the grass, half chewed, was expelled.

But she did not give up. There was a calf in her belly, sleeping calmly, trusting her to nurture it to the moment of its birth and then beyond. If she must train herself to live again, she would do it.

So she found more grass and kept trying, until she managed to keep some food in her stomach.

When she had eaten, she found a natural hollow in the ground. She reached over her shoulder for the skins and laid the pathetic remnants at the base of the hole.

She spent long heartbeats touching the skins with her trunk, trying to Remember Eggtusk, and the ancient mammoths from whom these skins had been stolen. But the strange odourless texture of the Lost lay over the skins; and the way they had been scraped and dried, punctured and stitched together, made them seem deeply unnatural.

There was little of Eggtusk left here.

When it was done she limped around the hollow, rumbling her mourning, and poked at the low mound of remains.

She longed to stay here, and she longed to sleep.

But she could feel her strength dissipating, even as she stood here. She had to return to the Family: to tell them what had become of Snagtooth and mighty Eggtusk, and to help Owlheart with whatever the matriarch decided they must do.

She turned to the north and began the long walk home.

*

She was a boulder of flesh and bone and fur that stomped stolidly over this blooming summer land, ignoring the shimmering belts of flowers, oblivious to the lemmings she startled from their burrows. As she walked, the warm wind from the south blew the last of her winter coat off her back, so that hair coiled into the air like spindrift from the sea.

She might have looked sullen, for she walked with her head lowered. But this is the habit of mammoths; Silverhair was inspecting the vegetation for the richest grass, which she cropped as often as she could manage.

But the food clogged in her throat as if it were a ball of hair and dirt. Her dung was hard and dry, sharp with barely digested grass. And the cold, though diminishing as the summer advanced, seemed to pierce her deeply.

Her sleep was fragmented, snatches she caught while shivering against rock outcrops, fearful of wolves and Lost.

The world map in her head was now more of a curse than a blessing. She could imagine the scope and rocky sweep of the Island, sense – from their contact rumbles and stamping – where the Family was clustered, far to the north.

She was just a pebble against this bitter panorama. And her own mind and heart – cluttered with the agonised memories of Eggtusk and Snagtooth and Lop-Ear, and with dread visions of the Lost and their light-bird, and with hopes and fears for the growing child inside her – were dwarfed, made insignificant by the pitiless immensity of the land.

As the sun wheeled in the sky she felt as if her contact with the world was loosening, as if the heavy pads of her feet were leaving the ground; she was a mammoth turning as light as the pollen of the tundra flowers which bloomed around her.

A storm descended.

A black cloud closed around her. The wind seemed to slap at her, each gust a fresh, violent blow. Her fur was plastered against her face. The ice dust hurled by the wind was sharp and dug into her flesh. She could see barely more than a few paces; she was driving herself through a bubble of light that fluctuated around her.

The storm blew out. But her strength was severely sapped.

She felt she could march no more.

She stopped, and let the sun's warmth play on her back.

After the storm, they sky was cloaked with a thin overcast. The sun's light was diffused, so that the air shimmered brightly all around her, and nothing cast a shadow. The sun, high to the north, shone faintly through the haze, and was flanked by a ghostly pair of sun dogs, reflections from ice crystals in the air.

The shadowless light was opalescent, very strange and beautiful.

She wasn't sure where she was, which way she should go. But she could smell water here; there was a stream, and pools of icemelt, and the grass grew thickly.

It was a good place to stay. Perhaps her dung would help this place flourish.

On a ground carpeted with bright-yellow Arctic daisies, she sank to her knees. The pain in her legs ceased to clamour. She would feed soon, and drink. But first she would sleep.

She rested her tusks on the ground and closed her eyes. She could feel the spin of the rocky Earth which bore her through space, sense it carry her beneath the brightness of the sun.

But there was a deeper cold beneath, a cold that was sucking at her.

Something made her open her eyes.

She saw a strange animal, standing unnaturally on its hind legs, brandishing a stick at her. In its paws it held something that glittered like ice, small and sharp.

And now she felt a nudging around her body, under her spine and at her buttocks. Irritated, she raised her head.

A huge Bull was trying to dig his tusks under her belly. *By the oozing scabs of Kilukpuk's cracked and bleeding moles, but you're a heavy great boulder of a Cow, little Silverhair. Come on – come—*

She tried to ignore him. After all, he wasn't real. 'Go away,' she said.

But we can't, you see, child. Another mammoth – this time a massive, ancient Cow who moved stiffly, as if plagued by arthritis – stood at her other side. *It isn't your day to die. Don't you know that? Your story isn't done yet.* And she tugged at Silverhair's tusks with her trunk.

Silverhair reluctantly got to her feet. 'I'm comfortable here,' she mumbled.

You never would listen. Another voice, somewhere behind her. Turning her head sluggishly, Silverhair saw this was a strange Cow indeed, with one shattered tusk and a trunk severed close to the root. The Cow was lowering her head and butting at Silverhair's buttocks, trying to nudge her forward.

The others, the Bull and the ancient Cow, had clustered to either side of her. They were huddling her, she realised.

Silverhair took a single, resentful step. 'I just want to be left alone.'

The Bull growled. *If you don't stop squealing like a calf, I'll paddle your behind. Now move.*

So, one painful step after another, her trunk dangling over the ground, Silverhair walked on. She leaned on one reassuring flank, and then the other; and the gentle nudging of the mutilated head behind her impelled her forward.

And the strange animal that walked upright stalked alongside her, just beyond reach of the mammoths, and his strange sharp objects glinted in his paw.

*

But it was not over. Still the land stretched ahead of her, curving over the limb of the planet.

Sometimes she thought she heard contact rumbles, and her hopes would briefly lift. But the sound was remote, uncertain, and she couldn't tell if it was real or just imagination.

She came to a place of frost heave, where ice domes as high as her belly had formed in the soil, ringed by shattered rock. This land was difficult to cross, and there was little food, for nothing could grow here.

One by one, the mammoths who had escorted her fell away: the ancient Cow, the crusty old Bull, the mutilated face that had bumped encouragingly at her rump.

Even the faint trace of contact rumbles died away. Perhaps it had only been thunder.

At last she was alone with the animal that walked upright. It glided beside her, as effortless as a shadow, waiting for her to fall.

She staggered on until the frost heave was behind her.

She stopped, and looked around dimly. She had come to a plain of black volcanic rock, barely broken even by lichen. It was a hard, uncompromising land: no place for the living.

She knelt once more, and let her chest sink to the ground, and then her tusks, which supported her head.

Here, then, she thought. Here it ends.

There was nobody here, no scent of mammoth on this barren land: no one to perform the Remembering ceremony for her and her calf. Well, then, she must do it for herself. She cast about with her trunk. But there was nothing to be had – no twigs or grass – nothing save a few loose stones, scattered over this bony landscape. She picked those up and dropped them on her back. Then she reached to her belly and tore out some hair, and scattered it over her spine.

. . . Silverhair . . . Silverhair . . .

There was a mammoth before her, tugging at her trunk.

She pulled back impatiently. 'Go away,' she mumbled. She had had enough of meddling ghosts.

But this mammoth was small, and it seemed to hop about before her, touching her trunk and mouth and tusks. *Silverhair, is it really you? Silverhair . . . Silverhair . . .*

'Silverhair.'

It was her nephew, Croptail. And beyond him she could see the great boulder shape of Owlheart, a cloud of flesh and fur and tusk.

She could smell them. They were real. Relief flooded her, and a great weakness fell on her, making her tremble.

She looked around, meaning to warn Owlheart about the strange upright-walking animal. But, for now, it had vanished.

Foxeye stroked her back and touched her mouth and trunk, and brought her food and water. Owlheart tended her wounds, stripping off the mud Silverhair had plastered there, washing the deepest of the cuts and covering them once more with fresh mud. She laid her trunk against Silverhair's belly hair, listening to the small life that was growing within. Even Croptail helped, in his clumsy way.

But the little one, Sunfire, was too young even to remember her aunt; the calf stood a few paces away from this battered, bloody stranger, her eyes wide as the Moon.

Later, Silverhair would marvel at Owlheart's patience. The Matriarch must have been bursting with questions. Yet, as the sun completed many cycles in the sky, Owlheart allowed Silverhair to reserve all her energy for recovery.

Silverhair tried to understand what had happened to her on the long walk home, but even as she tried to recall fragments of it, they would slip away, like bees from a flower.

She did wonder, though, why there hadn't been a fourth ghost out there helping her: a young Bull with a damaged ear . . .

At last Owlheart came to her.

'You know you've been lucky. A couple of those wounds on your legs were down to the very bone. But now you're healing. Kilukpuk must be watching over you, child.'

Silverhair raised her trunk wearily. 'I wish she'd watch a bit more carefully then.'

'How much do you remember?'

'Everything – I think – until those Lost captured me and tied my legs to the stakes. After that it gets a little blurred. Until Snagtooth—'

'Start at the beginning.'

And so, in shards and fragments, Silverhair told the Matriarch her story.

When she was done, Owlheart was grim. 'It is just as it says in the Cycle. It was like this in the time of Longtusk, when the Lost would wait for us to die, then eat our flesh, and shelter from the rain in caves made of our skin, and burn our bones for warmth. And they will not stop there. They will take more and more, their twisted hunger never sated.'

'Then what should we do?'

Owlheart raised her trunk and sniffed the air. 'For a long time we have been sheltered, here on this Island, where few Lost ever came. But now they know we are here we can only flee.'

'Flee? But where?'

Owlheart turned her face away from the sun, and the ice-laden wind whipped at her fur.

'North,' she said. 'We must go north, as mammoths always have.'

Chapter Two

THE GLACIERS

The migration began the next day.

Owlheart allowed many stops, for feeding and resting and passing dung; and when the midnight sun rolled along the horizon they slept. But when the mammoths moved, Owlheart had them sweep across the tundra at a handsome pace. They ran in the thin warmth of the noon sun, and they ran in the long shadows of midnight.

Foxeye shepherded her calf Sunfire, coaxing her to feed and pass dung and sleep. Croptail strayed further afield. He would dash ahead of the rest, pawing at the grass and rock with his trunk, and run in wide circles around the group, as if to deter any wolves. Owlheart caught Silverhair's eye, and an unspoken message passed between the Cows. *He's following his instinct. What he's doing is the right thing for a young Bull. But keep an eye on him; he's no Eggtusk yet.*

It was the height of summer now. The air above the endless bogs hummed with millions of gnats, midges, mosquitoes. The mosquitoes would hover in smoke-like dancing columns, before homing in on a mammoth's body heat with remarkable accuracy, until their victim was smothered by an extremely uncomfortable cloak of insect life. Blackflies were almost as much of a pest as mosquitoes, for they seemed able to penetrate the most dense layers of fur in their search for exposed skin – not just the soft parts, but even the harder skin of Silverhair's feet. They would stab their mouthparts through the skin to suck out the blood that sustained them, and the poison they injected into Silverhair's skin to keep the blood flowing freely caused swelling and intolerable itching.

But even the mosquitoes and flies were but a minor irritant to Silverhair, as her strength gradually returned. Mammoths are not designed to be still. Silverhair found that the hours of easy movement, her muscles strengthening and her wounds healing, smoothed the pain out of her body. Even her digestion improved as the steady, normal flow of food and water through her body was restored; soon her dung passed easily and was rich and thick once more.

And as they ran, it was as if more ghosts clustered around her: this time not just two or three or four mammoths, but whole Families, young and old, Bulls and calves, running together as smoothly as the grass of the tundra ripples in the wind. It seemed to Silverhair that their rumbles were merging, sinking into the ground, so that it was as if the whole plain undulated with the mammoths' greeting calls.

But then the ghosts would fade, and Silverhair would be left alone with her diminished Family: just three Cows, one immature Bull and a suckling infant, where once millions of mammoths had roamed across the great plains.

And so, once again, the Family approached the Mountains at the End of the World.

Sheets of hard black volcanic rock thrust out of the soil. No trees grew here; nothing lived but straggling patches of grass and lichen that clung to the frost-cracked rocks. The last of the soil was frozen hard, as if winter never left this place, and the rock was slick with ice.

At last they reached the lower slopes of the Mountains themselves. Rock rose above them, dwarfing even Owlheart, the tallest of the mammoths; Silverhair could see how the rock face had been carved and shattered by frost. And the clamour of ice and shattering rock was deafening for the mammoths, making it impossible for them to sense what might lie beyond.

They walked in the lee of the Mountains, until they came to a great glacier. It lay in a valley gouged through the rock, just as a mammoth's tongue lies in her jawbone. The ice at the glacier's snout lay in greying, broken heaps across the frozen ground. But beyond, to the north, the glacier was a ribbon of dazzling white, a frozen river that disappeared into the mist of the Mountains, and it seemed to draw the staring Silverhair with it.

Foxeye said, 'We shouldn't be here. This isn't a place for mammoths. The Cycle says so . . .'

'*There is a way through the Mountains*,' said Owlheart.

'How do you know?' asked Foxeye.

Owlheart said, 'Wolfnose – my Matriarch – once told me a time when *she* was but a calf, and the Matriarch then had memories of long before . . . There was a Bull calf with more curiosity than sense. Rather like you, Silverhair. He went wandering off by himself. He followed a glacier into the Mountains, and he said it broke right through the Mountains to the northern side. Although he didn't follow it to its end—'

Suddenly Owlheart's audacious plan was clear to Silverhair. She stood before the glacier, awed. 'So this is a path broken through the Mountains by the ice. Just as mammoths will break a path through a forest.'

'And that's where we're going,' said Owlheart firmly. 'We're going beyond the Mountains at the End of the World, where no mammoth has ventured before—'

'And for good reason.' Foxeye rocked to and fro, stamping on the hard ground. 'Because it's impossible, no matter what that rogue calf said. *If* he ever existed. We don't even know what's there, land or sea or ice—'

For a heartbeat Owlheart's resolve appeared to waver. She seemed to slump, as if she were ageing through decades in an instant.

Silverhair laid her trunk on Foxeye's head. 'Enough,' she said gently. 'We must follow the Matriarch, Foxeye.'

Foxeye subsided. But her unhappiness was obvious.

Owlheart nodded to Silverhair. Her unspoken command was clear: Silverhair was to lead the way.

Heart pumping, Silverhair turned, and stepped on to the ice.

Mammoths do not spend much of the time on the bare ice, because there is no food to be had there; their habitat is the tundra. But Silverhair understood the glacier, from experience and lore.

At first she walked over cracked-off fragments of ice scattered over the rock. But soon, as she worked her way steadily forward, she found herself walking on a continuous sheet of ice. It was hard and cold under the pads of her feet, but she had little difficulty maintaining her footing.

But it was *cold*. The sun was warm on one side of her, but the immense mass of ice seemed to suck the heat from the other side of her body and her belly, and she could feel a wide and uncomfortable temperature difference from one side to the other.

She was climbing a steepening blue-white hillside, which rose above her. She enjoyed the crunchy texture of the snow underfoot. Lumps of blue ice pushed out of the snow around her, carved by the wind into fantastic shapes. Here and there shattered ice lay in fans across the white surface she was climbing. The glacier was a river of ice, seemingly motionless around her, but its downhill flow was obvious nonetheless. Lines of scoured-off rock in the ice surface marked the glacier's millennial course. The glacier's shuddering under her feet was continuous, and Silverhair could feel its agonisingly sluggish progress through its valley, and could hear the low-pitched grind and crack of the compressed ice as it forced its way through the rock, and the high-pitched scream of the rock itself being shattered and torn away.

She came to a place where the thickening ice was split by crevasses. When it flowed out of the mountains onto the tundra the glacier was able to spread out, like a stream splashing over a plain, and so it cracked open. Most of the crevasses followed the line of the glacier as it poured down its gouged-out channel in the rock. But some of them, more treacherous, cut across the line of the flow.

Most of the crevasses were narrow enough to step across. Some were bridged by tongues of ice, but Silverhair tested these carefully before leading the mammoths on to them. If a crevasse was too wide she would guide the mammoths along its length until it was narrow enough to cross in safety.

She looked into one deep crevasse. The walls were sheer blue ice, broken here and there only by a small ledge or a few frost crystals. The crevasse was cluttered by the remains of collapsed snow bridges, but past them she could see the crevasse's endless depth, the blue of the ice becoming more and more intense until it deepened to indigo and then to darkness.

In some places, where the glacier had lurched downwards, there were icefalls: miniature cliffs of ice, like frozen waterfalls.

These were difficult to climb, especially where there were crevasses along the icefalls. And in some places where the glacier flowed awkwardly around a rock outcrop, the ice was shattered to blocks and shards by the shear stresses, and was very difficult to cross.

After a time, as the mammoths climbed up from the plain, there were fewer crevasses, and the going got easier. In some places the glacier was covered with hard white snow, but in others Silverhair found herself walking on clean blue unbroken ice. The blue ice wasn't flat, but was dimpled with cups and ridges. There were even frozen ripples here, their edges hard under her feet. It was exactly like walking over the frozen surface of a river.

When she looked back she could see the Family following in a ragged line: Foxeye with her two calves, and Owlheart bringing up the rear. They looked like hairy boulders, uncompromisingly brown against the blinding white of the ice.

She came to a chasm the glacier had cut deep into the mountain's rock. The mammoths were silent, even the calves, as they threaded through this cold, gloomy passage. Walls of hard blue-black rock towered above Silverhair. She could see scratches etched into the rock, and scattered over the ice there was sand, gravel, rocks, even boulders ripped out of place by the scouring ice.

At last the chasm opened out. Silverhair stepped forward cautiously, blinking as she emerged from the shadows.

She was surrounded by mountains.

She was on the lip of a natural bowl in the mountain range, a bowl which brimmed with ice; the mountain peaks, crusted with snow which would never melt, protruded above the ice like the half-buried tusks of some immense giant. The ice was trying to flow down to the plain below, but the mountains got in the way. The glaciers were the places where the ice leaked out. There were rings of frozen eddies and ripples, even waves, where the ice was pressing against the mountains' stubborn black rock faces.

The mammoths walked cautiously on to the ice bowl. There was nothing moving here but themselves, nothing before them but the plain of white ice, black rock, blue sky. But there was noise here: the distant cracks and growls and splintering crashes of ice avalanches, as great sheets broke away from the rocky faces all around them, a remote, vast, intimidating clamour. It was a clean, cold, silent place, white sprinkled with rugged black outcrops, the only smells the sharp tang of ice and the freezing musk of the mammoths themselves.

Silverhair heard her own breathing, and the squeak of the ice as it compressed under her feet. She felt small and insignificant, dwarfed by the majesty of her planet.

Owlheart stood alongside her. She was breathing hard after the climb, and her breath steamed around her face. 'Just as the Cycle describes it. From the ice which pools here, the glaciers flow to the tundra.'

'And,' said Silverhair, 'no mammoth has ever gone further north than this.'

'No mammoth before today. *Look*.'

Silverhair followed the Matriarch's gaze. She saw that on the northern horizon the mountains were marked by a notch: another valley scoured out by glaciers. And beyond, she could see blue-grey sky.

'That's our way through,' said Owlheart.

Silverhair reached the ravine on the far side of the ice bowl, and found herself standing on the creaking mass of another glacier.

She looked down the way she must climb.

The view was startling. The glacier was a frozen torrent sweeping down its valley, turning around a bluff in the rock before spreading, flattening and shattering to shards. The rubble lines along its length made the flow obvious. They ran in parallel, turning together with each curve of the glacier. They looked like wrinkles in stretched skin.

There were even tributary glaciers running into this main body, like streams joining a river. But where the tributaries merged, the ice was cracked into crevasses, or else shattered and twisted into fields of chaotic blocks.

Despite its stillness, she could see the drama of the great ice river's gush through the broken mountains, the endless battle between the stubborn rock and irresistible ice. Where the mountains constricted the flow, the ice reared up in great shattered, frozen whirlpools; and standing ice-waves lapped at the base of black hills, truncated by millennia of frost-shatter. She heard the roar of massive avalanches, the shriek of splitting rock, the groan of the shifting ice, and the sullen voice of the wind as it moaned through the valleys of rock and ice.

It was a panorama of white ice, black rock, blue sky.

The way forward would be difficult; she knew they would be fortunate to reach the northern lands without mishap. And yet her spirit was lifted by the majesty of the landscape. Despite her troubles and her pain, she felt profoundly glad to be alive: to have her small place in the great Cycle, to have come here and witnessed *this*.

She pressed on, stepping cautiously over the shattered ice.

At first the going, over a shallow snowdrift, was easy. But then the drift disappeared, without warning, and she found herself descending a slope of steep, slick blue ice. And as she climbed down further, the horizon increasingly dropped away from her, suggesting deep ice falls or steep and fissured drops ahead.

Climbing down a glacier turned out to be much harder than climbing up one had been.

At least on the way up she had been able to see the ice falls and crevasses before she reached them; here, even the biggest obstacles were invisible, hidden by the ice's sharp falling curve, until she was on them. And with every step she took, her feet either twisted in the meltpits that marked the ancient, ribbed blue ice, or else broke through a crust of ice, jarring her already aching joints.

She came to a moraine, an unbroken wall of boulders that lay across her path. The line of debris had been deposited on the surface of the ice by centuries of glacial flow. She picked her way through the boulders, flinching when her feet landed on frost-shattered rock chips.

Now she came to a place where the ice, constricted by two towering black cliffs to either side, was shattered, split by great crevasses. In the worst areas a confusion of stresses criss-crossed the ice with crevasse after crevasse, and the land became a chaotic wilderness of giant ice pillars, linked only by fragile snow bridges.

She crept through this broken place by sticking close to the cliff to her left-hand side. The ice here, clinging to the rock, was marginally less shattered. In some places she found clear runs of blue ice, which were easier to negotiate. But even these were a mixed blessing, for the ice was ridged and hard under her feet – and it had been kept clear only by the action of a scouring wind, and when that wind rolled off the ice bowl behind her it drove billows of ice crystals into her eyes, each gust a slap.

Then she was past the crevasse field, and the rock walls opened out . . . and for the first time she could see the northern lands.

It was a plain of ice – nothing but ice, studded with trapped bergs, dotted here and there with the blue of water.

Her heart sank.

The glacier decanted on to a rocky shore littered with broken stone and scraps of ice. She walked forward. This might have been the twin of the Island's southern coast. The landfast ice was more thickly bound to the ground here than in the south, but she could see leads of clear water and dark steam clouds above them. There was no sign of vegetation, no grass or bushes or trees – nor, indeed, any exposed rock. Nothing but ice: a great sheet of it, over which nothing moved.

A huge floe was drifting close to the shore, and, cautiously, she stepped on to it. It tipped with a grand slowness, and she heard the crunch of splintering ice at its edge. The floe was pocked by steaming air-holes, through which peered the heads of seals.

As she watched, a seal reared out of the water to strike at an incautious diving sea bird, dragging it into the ocean. There was a swirl, a final, despairing squawk, and the seal's head erupted from the water with the bird's body crushed between its jaws. Then the seal thrashed its head from side to side with stunning violence, tearing the bird to pieces, literally shaking it out of its skin.

It was not a promising welcome for the mammoths, Silver-hair thought.

Some distance to the west, a glacier was pushing its way into the sea ice. The pressure had made the ice fold up into great ridges around the tongue of the glacier, and in the depressions between the wind-smoothed ridges ice blocks had heaped up. At the tip of the glacier there was a sudden explosion, and a vast cloud of powdered snow shot up into the air. The roaring noise continued, and as the snow cleared a little, she saw that the snout of the glacier was splitting away, a giant ravine cracking its way down the thickness of the ice river, and a pinnacle of ice tipping away from the glacier, towards the sea. It was the long, stately birth of a new iceberg. In the low light of the sun the snow was pink, the new berg a deep sky-blue.

She could feel the ocean swelling beneath her feet, heard the groan of the shifting ice. The sky was empty save for the deep grey-blue of the far north, the colour of cold.

And she knew now that the ocean beneath her feet swept all the way to the north: all the way to the axis of the Earth.

Owlheart climbed aboard the floe beside her, making it rock. 'It's a frozen ocean,' the Matriarch said.

'Yes. We can't live here.'

'I feared as much,' said Owlheart. Her rumble was complex, troubled. 'But . . .'

Silverhair, uncertainly, wrapped her trunk around Owlheart's. She was not accustomed to comforting a Matriarch. 'I know. You had no choice but to try.'

'And now,' said Owlheart bitterly, 'at the fringe of this cursed frozen sea, we have nowhere to go.'

There was a distant clattering sound, intermittent, carried on the wind. Silverhair turned.

Something – complex, black and glittering – was flying along the beach from the west. Sweeping directly towards Foxeye and her calves. Sending a clattering noise washing over the ice.

It was the light-bird of the Lost.

Chapter Three

THE CHASM OF ICE

The light-bird clattered over their heads like a storm. Owlheart reared up and pawed at the air. There was a stink of burning tar, a wash of downrushing wind from those whirling wings that drove the hair back from Silverhair's face. She could see Lost – two, three of them – cupped in the bird's strange crystal belly, staring down at her.

Silverhair and Owlheart hurried back to the shore, where Foxeye and her calves were waiting, cowering.

A faint scent of burning came to them on the salty breeze. The calves, huddling close to their mother, picked it up immediately; they raised their little trunks and trumpeted in alarm.

Silverhair looked along the beach, to the west, the way the bird had come. She could see movement, a strange dark rippling speckled with light. And there was a cawing, like gulls.

It was the Lost: a line of them, spread along the beach. And the light was the yellow fire of torches which they carried in their paws.

Owlheart rumbled and trumpeted; Silverhair had never seen her so angry. 'They pursue us even *here*? I'll destroy them all. I'll drag that monster from the sky and smash it to shards—'

Silverhair wrapped her trunk around the Matriarch's, and dragged her face forward. 'Matriarch. Listen to me. I've seen that light-bird before, at the camp of the Lost. It makes a lot of noise but it won't harm us. *There*—' She looked down the beach, at the approaching line of Lost. '*That* is what we must fear.'

'I will trample them like mangy wolves!'

'No. They will kill you before your tusks can so much as scratch them. *Think,* Matriarch.'

She could see the effort it took for Owlheart to rein in her Bull-like instincts to drive off these puny predators. 'Tell me what to do, Silverhair,' she said.

'We must run,' said Silverhair. 'We can outrun the Lost.'

'And then?' asked Owlheart bleakly.

'That is for tomorrow. First we must survive today,' said Silverhair bluntly.

'Very well. But, whatever happens today—' Owlheart tugged at Silverhair's trunk, urgently, affectionately. '*Remember me*,' she said, and she turned away.

Stunned, Silverhair watched the Matriarch's broad back recede.

The coastline here was mountainous. Black volcanic rock towered above the fleeing mammoths.

They came to another huge glacier spilling from the mountains, a cliff of ice that loomed over them. The beach was strewn with shattered ice blocks, and the glacier itself, a sculpture in green and blue, was cracked by giant ravines. The air which spilled down from within the ravines was damp and chill – cold as death, Silverhair thought.

They ran on, the three Cows panting hard, their breath steaming around their faces, the calves mewling and crying as their mother goaded them forward.

The cries of the Lost seemed to be growing louder, as if they were gaining. And still the light-bird clattered over their heads, its noise and tarry stink and distorted wind washing over them, driving them all close to panic.

Silverhair wished Lop-ear were here. He would know what to do.

Owlheart shuddered to a halt, staring along the beach. Foxeye and the calves, squealing, slowed behind her.

Silverhair came up to Owlheart. 'What is it?'

And now the wind swirled, and the stink reached Silverhair. A stink of flesh.

Strung across the beach was a series of heaps of stone and sand and ice. From each heap, oily black smoke rose up to the sky. The fire came from a thick dark substance plastered over the stones.

What burned there was mammoth.

Silverhair could smell it: bone and meat, and even some hair and skin, bound together by fat and dung. And one of the stone heaps was even crowned with a mammoth skull, devoid of flesh and skin and hair.

She recognised it immediately, and recoiled in horror and disgust. It was Eggtusk's skull.

Foxeye was standing still, shuddering. The two calves were staring wide-eyed at the fires, crying.

'We can't go through that,' growled Owlheart.

Silverhair was battling her own compulsion to flee this grisly horror. 'But we must. It's just stones and fire. We can knock those piles down, and—'

'No.' Owlheart trotted back a few paces and stared into the mouth of a great ravine in the glacier. 'We'll go this way.

Maybe we'll find a way through. At least the light-bird won't be able to chase us there.' She prodded Foxeye. 'Come on. Bring the calves.'

In desperation Silverhair plucked at Owlheart's tail. 'No. Don't you see? That's what they want us to do.'

Owlheart swiped at her with her tusks, barely missing Silverhair's scarred cheek. 'This is a time to follow me, Silverhair, not to question.'

And she turned her back, deliberately, and led her Family into the canyon of ice.

Silverhair looked along the beach. One of the Lost was standing on a boulder before the others, waving his spindly forelegs in a manner of command. Silverhair could see the ice light glint from his bare scalp. It was Skin-of-Ice: the monster of the south, come to pursue her, even here beyond the End of the World. She felt a black despair settle on her soul.

She followed her Matriarch into the ravine.

Immediately the air felt colder, piercing even the mammoths' thick coats. Immersed in ice, Silverhair felt the sting of frost in her long nostrils, and her breath crackled as it froze in the hair around her mouth.

Impatient to make haste, anxious to keep their footing, the mammoths filed through the chasm, furry boulder-shapes out of place in this realm of sculpted ice. The going was difficult; the ground was littered with slabs and blocks of cracked-off ice, dirty and eroded. With each step ice blocks clattered or cracked, and the sharp noises echoed in the huge silence.

Walls of ice loomed above Silverhair, sculpted by melt and rainfall into curtains and pinnacles. The daylight was reduced to a strip of blue-grey far above. But it wasn't dark here, for sunlight filtered through the ice, illuminating blue-green depths there.

It was almost beautiful, she thought.

Silverhair heard a clattering. She looked back to the mouth of the chasm. The light-bird hovered there, black and sinister. As Owlheart had predicted, it couldn't follow them here. Perhaps its whirling wings were too wide to fit within the narrow walls.

But on the ground she could see the skinny limbs of the Lost, the smoky light of their torches, as they clambered over ice blocks.

Owlheart had gone ahead of the others, deeper into the chasm. Now she returned, trumpeting her rage. 'There's no way out. A fall of ice has completely blocked the chasm.' She growled. 'Our luck is running out, Silverhair.'

'Luck has nothing to do with it,' said Silverhair. She felt awe: she was sure the Lost – in fact, Skin-of-Ice himself – were behind every element of this trap: the burning fat and the skull, the driving of the mammoths into this chasm, and now the barrier at its rear. How was it possible for a mind to be so twisted as to concoct such complex schemes?

Owlheart rumbled, paced back and forth, struck the ground with her tusks. 'We aren't done yet. Listen to me. In some places, at the back of the chasm, the ice lies thin over the rock. And the rock is rotten with frost. Silverhair, go up there and dig. See if you can find a way out. If there's a way, take Foxeye and the calves. Get away from here and join up with one of the other Families.'

'Where?'

'Find them, Silverhair. It's up to you now.'

'What about you?'

Owlheart turned to face the encroaching Lost, and their fire glittered in her deep-sunken eyes. 'The Lost will have to clamber over my bloated corpse before they reach our calves.'

'Owlheart—'

'It will make a good story in the Cycle, won't it?' The Matriarch tugged at Silverhair's trunk one last time, and touched her mouth and eyes. 'Go to work, Silverhair, and hurry; you might yet save us all.'

Then she turned and faced the advancing Lost.

Silverhair turned to Foxeye, who stood over her terrified calves. 'They're trying to suckle,' Foxeye said, her voice all but inaudible. 'But I have no milk to give them. I'm too frightened, Silverhair. I can't even give them milk . . .'

'It's all right,' Silverhair said. 'We'll get out of here yet.' But the words sounded hollow to her own ears.

'They've come to destroy us, haven't they? Maybe Snag-tooth was right. Maybe all we can do is throw ourselves on the mercy of the Lost.'

'The Lost *have* no mercy.'

Foxeye said bleakly, 'Then let them kill Owlheart, and spare me and my calves.'

Silverhair was shocked. 'You don't mean that. Listen to me. I'm going to save you. You and the calves. It isn't over yet, Foxeye; not while I have breath in my body.'

Foxeye hesitated. 'You promise?'

'Yes.' Silverhair shook her sister's head with her trunk. 'Yes, I promise. Wait here.'

She turned and ran, deeper into the chasm.

The ravine became so narrow that it would barely have admitted two or three mammoths abreast, and the wind, pouring down from the glacier above, was sharp with frost crystals. But Silverhair lowered her head and kept on, until she found the way jammed by the jumble of fallen ice Owlheart had described.

The blocks here were sharp-edged and chaotically cracked, as if they had been broken off the ice walls above by the scraping of some gigantic tusk. Silverhair stared at the impassable barrier, wondering how even the Lost could have caused damage on such a scale so quickly.

She turned and worked her way back down the chasm. At last she found a patch of blue-black rock protruding through the ice walls. Perhaps the strength of the wind here had kept this outcrop free of frost and snow. But it was some distance above her head.

Before it, on the ground, there was a mound of scree – frost-shattered stone – mixed with loose snow and ice.

She stepped forward. The scree crunched and slithered under her feet. It was very tiring, like climbing up a snow bank. Small rocks began to litter the ice floor, broken off the rock face by frost, increasing with size until she found herself climbing past giant boulders.

A thunder-stick cracked.

Its sharp noise rattled from the sheer walls of the chasm. And now the screams of terrified mammoths echoed from the walls.

Every fibre in her being impelled Silverhair to lunge back down the slope and return to her people. But she knew she must stick to her task.

She turned and resumed her climb.

When she could reach the rock face, Silverhair dug into the wall with her tusks. The rock was loosely bound and easily scraped aside. As Owlheart had predicted, the exposed rock was rotten. Water would seep into the slightest crack and then, on freezing, expand, so widening the crack. Lichen, orange and green, dug into the friable rock face, accelerating its disintegration. Gradually the rock was split open, in splinters, shards or great sheets, and over the years fragments had fallen away to form the slope of scree below her.

With growing urgency Silverhair ground her way deeper into the rotten rock. Soon she was working in a hail of frost-shattered debris, and she ignored the sharp flakes that dug into the soft skin of her trunk.

But the chasm was full of the screams of the calves, and she muttered and wept as she worked.

Then – quite suddenly – the wall fell away, and there was a deep, dark space ahead of her.

A cave.

Hope surged in her breast. With increased vigour she pounded at the rock face before her, using tusks, trunk, forehead, to widen the hole. The rock collapsed to a heap of frost-smashed rubble before her.

She reached forward with her trunk. There was no wall ahead of her. But she could feel the walls to either side, scratched and scarred. *Scarred* – by mammoth tusks? But how could that be, so deep under the ground?

There was a breath of air, blowing the hairs on her face. Air that stank of brine. Owlheart had been right; there must be a passage here, open to the air. And that was all that was important right now; mysteries of tusk-scraped walls could wait.

But would the passage prove too narrow to get through? She had to find out before she committed them all to a trap.

Scrambling over the broken rocks, she plunged into the exposed cavern. It extended deep into the rock face. There was no light here, but she could feel the cool waft of brine, hear the soft echo of her footfalls from the walls. She pushed deeper, looking for light.

And so it was that Silverhair did not see what became of Owlheart, as she confronted the troop of Lost.

The Lost advanced towards Owlheart, and their cries echoed from the walls.

The Matriarch reared up, raising her trunk and tusks, and

trumpeted. Her voice, magnified by the narrow canyon walls, pealed down over the Lost, sounding like a herd of a thousand mammoths. And when she dropped back to the ground, her forefeet slammed down so hard they shook the very Earth.

But the Lost continued to advance.

After that first explosion of noise, the Lost had lowered their thunder-sticks and piled them on the ground. But now they raised up other weapons.

Here was a stick with a shard of rib or tusk embedded in its end. Here was a piece of shoulder blade, its edge sharpened cruelly, so huge it all but dwarfed the Lost who clutched it. And here were simple splinters of bone, held in paws, ready to slash and wound.

A chill settled around her heart. For they were weapons made of mammoth bone.

She put aside her primitive fear and assembled a cold determination. Whatever these Lost intended with this game of bones and sticks, the battle would surely take longer – win or lose – than if they used the thunder-sticks. If Silverhair stayed where she was and carried out her orders, they would have a chance.

Now one of the Lost came towards her. He was holding up a stick tipped with a bone shard.

She lowered her head, eyeing him. 'So,' she told him, 'you are the first to die.'

She waited for him to close with her. That thin wooden stick would be no match for her huge curved ivory tusks. She would sweep it aside, and then—

The Lost hurled his stick as hard as he could.

Utterly unexpected, it flew at her like an angry bird. The bone tip speared through her chest, unimpeded by the hair and skin and new summer fat there. She could feel it grind against a rib, and pierce her lung.

Staggering, she tried to take a breath. But it was impossible, and there was a sucking feeling at her chest.

Oddly, there was little pain: just a cold, clean sensation.

But her shock was huge. The Lost hadn't even closed with her yet – *but she knew she had taken her last breath*. As suddenly as this, with the first strike, it was over.

The Lost who had injured her knew what he had done. He was jumping up and down, waving his paws in the air in triumph.

Well, she thought, if this breath in my lungs is to be my last, I must make it count.

She plunged forward and twisted her head. The sharp tip of her right tusk cut clean through the skin and muscle of the throat of the celebrating Lost.

He looked down in disbelief as his blood spilled out over his chest and fell to the ice, steaming. Then he fell, slipping in his own blood.

Owlheart charged again, and now she was in amongst the Lost.

She reached out with her trunk, and grabbed one of them around the waist. He screamed, flailing his arms, as she lifted him high into the air. While she held him up, another bone-tipped stick was hurled at her chest. It pierced her skin but hit a rib, doing little damage. Impatiently she crashed her chest against the ice wall. There was an instant of agonising pain as the embedded sticks twisted her wounds a little further open, but then they broke away.

She tightened the grip of her mighty trunk until she felt the Lost's thin bones crack; he shuddered in her grip, then turned limp. She dropped him to the ice.

She longed to take a breath, but knew she must not try.

Two dead. She knew she would not survive this encounter, but perhaps it wasn't yet over; if she could destroy one or two more of the Lost, Silverhair and the others might still have a chance.

She looked for her next opponent. They were strung out before her, wary now, shouting, raising their sticks and shoulder blades.

She selected one of them. She raised her trunk and charged. He dropped his stick, screamed and ran. She prepared to trample him.

. . . But now another came forward. It was the hairless one, the one Silverhair called Skin-of-Ice.

He hurled a stick.

It buried itself in her mouth with such venomous power that her head was knocked sideways.

She fell. The stick caught on the ground, driving itself further into the roof of her mouth. The agony was huge.

She tried to get her legs underneath her. She knew she must rise again. But the ground was slippery, coated with some slick substance. She looked down, and saw that it was her own blood; it soaked, crimson and thick, into the broken ice beneath her.

And now the hairless Lost stood before her. He held up a shard of bone, as if to show it to her.

She gathered her strength for one last lunge with her tusk. He evaded her easily.

He stepped forward and plunged the bone into her belly, ripping at skin and muscle. Coiled viscera, black with blood, snaked on to the ice from her slashed belly. She tried to rise, but her legs were tangled in something.

Tangled in her own spilled grey guts.

She fell forward. She raised her trunk. Perhaps she could trumpet a final warning. But her breath was gone.

Within her layers of fat and thick wool, Owlheart had

spent her life fighting the cold. But now, at last, her protection was breached. And the cold swept over her exposed heart.

In a cloud of rock dust, Silverhair burst out of her cavern, back into the chasm.

She was overwhelmed by the noise: the screams and trumpets of terrified mammoths, the calls and yelps of the Lost, the relentless clatter of the light-bird, all of it rattling from the sheer ice walls.

Owlheart had fallen.

Silverhair could see two of the Lost climbing over her flank. They were hauling bone-tipped sticks out of her side, and then plunging them deep into her again, as if determined to ensure she was truly dead.

But Owlheart had not given her life cheaply. Silverhair could see the unmoving forms of two of the Lost, broken and gouged.

Silverhair mourned her fallen Matriarch, and her courage. But it had not been enough. For the rest of the Lost were advancing towards Foxeye and the calves.

And Skin-of-Ice himself, bearing a giant stick tipped with sharpened bone, was leading them.

Foxeye seemed frozen by her fear. Sunfire, the infant, was all but invisible beneath the belly hairs of her mother. And Croptail, the young Bull, stepped forward; he raised his small trunk and brayed his challenge at the Lost.

Skin-of-Ice made a cawing noise, and looked to his companions. Silverhair, anger and disgust mixing with her fear, knew that the malevolent Lost, already stained with the blood of the Matriarch, was mocking the impossible bravery of this poor, trapped calf.

Silverhair raised her trunk and trumpeted. She started down

the scree slope. 'Croptail! Get your mother. We can escape. Come on—'

The Lost looked up, startled. Some of them seemed afraid, she thought with satisfaction, to see another adult mammoth apparently materialise from the solid rock wall.

Perhaps that pause would give her a chance to save her Family.

The young Bull ran to his mother. He tugged at her trunk until she raised her head to face him.

But the Lost were closing, raising their sticks and claws of bone. Silverhair saw how one of them broke and ran to the thunder-sticks at the mouth of the cave. But Skin-of-Ice barked at him, and he returned. Silverhair felt cold. This was a game to Skin-of-Ice, a deadly game he meant to finish with his shards of bone and wood.

Silverhair tried to work out what chance they had. The ground was difficult for the Lost; Silverhair saw how they stumbled on the slippery, ice-coated rock, and were forced to clamber over boulders and ice chunks that the mammoths, with their greater bulk, could brush aside. And once the Family were safely in the tunnel, Silverhair would emulate Owlheart. She would make a stand and disembowel any Lost who tried to follow—

But now the shadows flickered, and an unearthly clatter rattled from the ice and exposed rock. She looked up and flinched. The light-bird was hovering over the chasm.

Two of the Lost were leaning precariously out of the bird's gleaming belly. They were holding something, like a giant sheet of skin. They dropped it into the cavern. It fell, spreading out as it did so. Silverhair saw that it was like a spider-web – but a web that was huge and strong, woven from some black rope.

And, as the Lost had surely intended, the web fell neatly over Foxeye and her calves.

Foxeye's humped head pushed upwards at the web, and Silverhair could see the small, agitated form of Croptail. But the more the mammoths struggled, the more entangled they became. Sunfire's terrified squealing, magnified by the ice, was pitiful.

Silverhair started forward, trying to think. Perhaps she could rip the web open with her tusks—

But now there was a storm of thunder-stick shouts, a hail of the invisible stinging things they produced. Instinctively she scrambled up the scree slope to the mouth of her cave.

The fire came from the Lost leaning out of the belly of the light-bird. They were pointing thunder-sticks at her. Bits of rock exploded from the ground and walls.

Down in the chasm, the Lost were walking over the fallen webbing, holding it down with their weight where it appeared the mammoths might be breaking free. Skin-of-Ice himself clambered on top of Croptail's trapped, kneeling bulk. Almost casually, he probed through the net with his bone-tipped stick. Silverhair saw blood fount, and heard Croptail's agonised scream.

Her heart turned to ice.

. . . But the thunder-stick hail still slammed into the frost-cracked rock around her. Great shards and flakes flew into the air. She had no choice but to stumble back into her cave.

She trumpeted her defiance at the light-bird. As soon as the lethal hail diminished, she would charge.

But now there was a deeper rumbling, from above her head.

A great sheet of rock fell away from the chasm wall above the cave opening. Dust swirled over her. Then a huge chunk of the cave's roof separated and fell. She was caught in a vicious rain of rocks that pounded at her back and head, and the air became so thick with dust she could barely breathe.

Still she tried to press forward. But the falling rock drove her back, pace by pace, and the light of the chasm was hidden.

The last thing she heard was Foxeye's desperate, terrified wail. '*You promised me, Silverhair! You promised me!*'

Then, at last, Silverhair was sealed up in darkness and silence.

Chapter Four

THE CAVE OF SALT

Alone in the dark, Silverhair dug at the fallen boulders until she could feel the ivory of her tusks splintering against the unyielding rock, and blood seeped along her trunk from a dozen cuts and scrapes.

But the rocks, firmly wedged in place, were immovable.

She sank to her knees and rested her tusks on the invisible, uneven ground.

The calves had been captured – perhaps even now they were being butchered by the casually brutal Skin-of-Ice and his band of Lost. What was left for her now?

In the depths of her despair, she looked for guidance. And she found it in the last orders of her Matriarch.

She must seek out her Cousins: the other Families that had made up the loose-knit Clan of the Island, a Clan that had once been part of an almost infinite network of mammoth blood alliances that had spread around the world. Her way forward was clear.

. . . But what, a small voice prompted her, if there *were* no more Families to be found? What if the worst fears of Wolfnose and Lop-ear had come true?

She tried to imagine discovering such a terrible thing: how she would feel, what she would do.

She would, simply, have to cope, find a way to go on. For now she had her orders from the Matriarch, and she would follow them. And besides, she had a promise to her sister to keep.

But first she had to get out of this cave.

With new determination she got to her feet, shook off the dust which had settled over her coat, and turned her head, seeking the breeze.

The cave was completely dark.

She moved with the utmost caution, her trunk held out before her. Her progress was slow. The floor was broken and uneven, the passage narrow and twisting, and she was afraid she might stumble over jagged rock or tumble into an unseen ravine.

And fear crowded her imagination. Mammoths, creatures of the open tundra, are not used to being enclosed; Silverhair tried not to think about the weight of rock and ice and soil that was suspended over her head.

But the echoes of her footsteps, crunching on ancient gravel, gave her a sense of a passageway stretching ahead of her. And there was the breeze: the slightest of zephyrs, laden with the sour stink of brine, somehow worming its way through cracks in the ground to this buried place.

And the breeze grew stronger, little by little, as she progressed.

But the passageway took her downwards.

As she moved deeper into the belly of the Earth, the air began to grow warmer. She heard the slow dripping of water from the walls, felt the channels those tiny drips had carved in the rock at her feet over the Great-Years. She licked the droplets from the wall. The water was cool and only a little salty, but there wasn't enough of it to quench her thirst.

At first the rising heat was comfortable – preferable, anyhow, to the dry, deathly chill of the ice chasm. Suspended here in the dark, she tried to imagine she was feeling the sun on her back, rather than the soulless, sourceless heat of deep rock.

But soon the warmth became less pleasant. She felt her heart race. She spread her ears as far as they would go, lifted her tail and opened her anus flap, opened her mouth and extended her tongue: all devices to let her body heat escape into this cloying air.

On she walked, deeper and deeper into the dark, and still the heat gathered.

At last the breeze felt a little cooler, and the quality of the echoes from the tunnel ahead changed. Underfoot the ground sloped, suddenly, much more sharply downwards.

She stopped.

The passage here, she sensed, broadened out into a wider cave. The mouth of her tunnel was set a little way above the floor of the cave. She extended her head and trunk into the empty space beyond the tunnel. The air here was much cooler, and she dropped her ears and anus flap.

With great care she worked her way down a shallow slope of scree to the floor of the cave.

She was still in complete darkness, but she could sense the great dome of this cave's ceiling far above her, like the roof of some giant mouth.

The breeze seemed to be coming from the opposite side of the cave. But she felt wary of striking out into the darkness.

So she began to feel her way along the wall.

The soft, gritty rock here was extensively scratched and

scoured. She ran the sensitive tip of her trunk over furrows and grooves.

They were unmistakably the marks of mammoth tusks.

The scrapings of tusks were everywhere, even – she suspected – higher than she could reach herself. She imagined huge old Bulls reaching high up with their gigantic tusks to bring down fresh rock for their Families.

When she ventured a few paces away from the wall, she found the uneven floor littered with mammoth dung. It was obvious that the whole of this cavern had been shaped by the working of mammoths, over generations. But when she picked up some of the dung and broke it open, it crumbled, dry as dust. It was very old, and it was evident that no mammoth had been here for many years.

She used her own tusk to scrape free pebble-sized lumps of rock from the wall. She picked them up, tucked them in her mouth, ground them to sand with her huge teeth and swallowed them. The rock's flavour was deliciously sharp: perhaps born from an ancient volcano, this loose, ash-like rock was evidently rich in salt and other minerals the mammoths needed.

The reason for the mammoths' presence here was clear. Mammoths need salt and other minerals, as do other animals. But their tongues are not long enough to reach around their trunks and tusks to salt-licks, exposed outcroppings of salty minerals. So they dig them up, using their tusks to loosen the earth. This whole cavern system might once have been a simple seam of soft, salty rock into which the mammoths had dug, until at last they had shaped this giant cave and the tunnels that led to it.

Silverhair held fragments of the rock on her tongue, relishing the salty taste and the rich, ancient mammoth smell of the place, as if she were tasting the living past itself. She walked on, surrounded by the workings of her ancestors, obscurely comforted.

At last she came to a heap of scree. The fresh breeze seemed to be spilling from a hole somewhere above her head. It must be another tunnel.

She clambered on to the scree. Her feet scrabbled to get a foothold in the unstable mass; it took several efforts before she had raised herself sufficiently to get her forelegs over the lip of the tunnel. But then it was a simple matter to pull herself all the way in.

She turned her back on the salt cave and marched on, into the darkness.

She felt the tunnel floor rising. The walls closed around her uncomfortably; if she took a step to either side she brushed against warm rock. But, as she climbed, she felt a delicious, welcoming chill return to the air. The breeze she had followed continued to strengthen.

And, ahead of her now, she made out splinters of green-blue light.

Gradually, as her eyes adapted better, she saw that the pale-green glow was outlining the walls and floor and roof of her tunnel. She could even make out the larger boulders on the floor, and she was able to press forward with confidence.

At last she came to a new chamber. Like the first she had found, this chamber had evidently been hollowed out by mammoths. But this one was flooded with light. The low rocky roof had collapsed. She could see great slabs of rock scattered over the floor, gouged cruelly by the ice, and only spires and pinnacles of rock remained. But the cave was enclosed by a roof of ice.

In some places the ice was smooth and bare. Elsewhere the roof was made of snow, with thick white pillars and balls of ice crusting its under-surface, all of it glowing blue-white. Some of the roof ice had broken off and pieces of it lay scattered over the floor with the rock chunks. Perhaps this was an outlying tongue of a glacier, strong enough to bridge this hole in the ground, thin enough to let through the light.

But the light was very dim here. The sunlight was scattered by the ice and turned to a deep, extraordinary blue, translucent, richer than any colour she had seen before. Silverhair wouldn't have been surprised to see Siros, the water-loving calf of Kilukpuk, come swimming through the air towards her, her legs reduced to stubby flippers.

She worked her way around the gouged walls.

Most of the scouring was functional: simple scrapes, often ending in a ragged scar where a chunk of the salty rock had been prised away. But some of the gouging here was strange. There were marks that were small and grouped in compact patterns, and they seemed to have been made with a great deal of care. At the base of the wall she found pebbles – and even a chipped-off piece of tusk – that looked as if they had been picked up and used to mould the gouges just so.

As she stared at them, the patterns were somehow familiar.

Here was a simple series of down-scrapes – but for a heartbeat Silverhair could *see*, as if looking beyond the scrapes, a dogged mammoth standing alone in a winter storm, thick winter hair dangling around her. And here two little clusters of scrapes became a Cow with her calf, who suckled busily.

But then she lost the images, like losing her grasp on a lush strand of grass, and there were only crude gouges in the salty rock.

These markings came from a richer time: a time when there were so many mammoths on the Island they were forced to dig far underground in search of salty rock, and they were so secure they had the time and energy to record their thoughts and dreams in scrapings on the walls. It must have taken a Great-Year to make these caves, she thought; but the mammoths (before *now*, at any rate) had never been short of time.

If only she understood what she was seeing, she thought, she might find the wisdom of another Cycle here: not songs passed down from mother to calf, but messages locked for ever in the face of the rock. Lop-ear would surely have understood these images: she remembered the way he had scraped at the frost, making markings to show her the Island as a bird would see it. Lop-ear would have been happy here, she realised: happy surrounded by the frozen thoughts of his ancestors.

But all the dung was dry and odourless, very old; and the wall markings were coated by layers of hardy lichen, orange and green, fuelling their perennial growth with ice-filtered light.

It had been the scraping of mammoths that had opened up the passages she followed, even the underground caves she had found. And now it was the patient work of those long-gone mammoths that was providing her with a means of escape from the Lost. Had they known, as they dug and shaped the Earth, that their actions would have such dramatic consequences for the future?

Encouraged by the presence of her ancestors, she walked on into the dark, and the gathering breeze.

And, after only a little more time, she emerged from a rocky mouth into summer daylight.

The fresh air and the light brought her relief, but no joy.

She clung to Owlheart's instructions about seeking out help, about joining with another Family, if it could be found. So she began a wide detour towards the south-east of the Island. There was a place she had visited as a calf, many years ago, where the land was hummocky and uneven, and there were many deep, small ponds. Here – held the wisdom of the Clan –

even in the hardest winter, it was often possible to smash through the thinner ice with a blow from a tusk, and reach liquid water.

And here, she hoped, she would find signs of the other Families of the Clan: if not the mammoths themselves, then at least evidence that they had been here recently, and maybe some clue about which way they had gone, and where she could find them.

If not here, she thought grimly, then nowhere.

But as she worked her way south, still she saw no signs of other mammoth Families.

She walked on, doggedly.

The tundra was still alive with flowers. There were bright-purple saxifrages, mountain avens studded with white flowers, and cushions of moss campion with their tiny white blossoms. Silverhair found a cluster of Arctic poppies, their cup-shaped yellow heads turning to the sun; they were drenched with dew where a summer fog had rolled over them, bringing them valuable moisture. Even on otherwise barren ground, the grass grew thick and green around the mouths of Arctic fox burrows, places fed by dung and food remains perhaps for centuries.

All the plants were adapted to the extreme cold, dryness and searing winds of the Island. They grew in clumps: tussocks, carpets and rosettes, and their leaves were thick and waxy, which helped them retain their water.

But already the summer was past its peak.

The insect life was dying back. The hordes of midges, mosquitoes and blackflies were gone; the adults, having laid their eggs long ago, were all dead, leaving the larvae to winter in the soil or pond water. Spiders and mites were seeking shelter in the soil or the litter of decaying lichen and vegetation.

Birth, a brief life of light and struggle, rapid death. Silverhair sensed the mass of the baby inside her, and her heart was heavy. Would she be able to give her own child even as much as this, as the short lives of the summer creatures?

Through the briefly teeming landscape, oblivious to the riot of colour, Silverhair walked stolidly on.

Seeking to build up her strength for whatever lay ahead, she took care to feed, drink and pass dung properly. Feeding was, briefly, a pleasure at this time of year, for the berries were ripe. She munched on the bright-red cranberries, yellow cloudberries, midnight-blue bilberries and inky-black crowberries which clustered on leathery plants. But there was a tinge of sadness about this treat, for the ripening berries were another sign of the autumn that was already close.

After a few days she could hear the soft lapping of water, smell the thick scummy greenness of the life that gathered in the deep ponds of this corner of the Island.

But there was still no sign of mammoth: no stomping, no contact rumbles, no smell of fur and milk.

And at last she came to the place of the ponds, and her heart sank. For she found herself treading on the bones of a young mammoth.

When he died he – or she – must have been about the same age as Croptail. The scavengers and the frost had left little of the youngster's skin and fur, and the cartilage, tendon and ligament had been stripped from the bones, which were separated and scattered. Some of the bones bore teeth marks, and some had been broken open, she saw, by a wolf or fox eager to suck the nourishing, fatty marrow from inside.

He must have been dead for months.

She touched the scattered bones with her feet, in a brief moment of Remembering. But she knew she could not linger here. For ahead of her – between herself and the glimmering surface of the ponds – there was a field full, she saw now, of stripped and scattered bones.

She walked forward with caution and dread.

Soon there were so many bones, so badly scattered, it was impossible even to pick out individuals. But still, she could see from their size that most of those who had died here had been youngsters – even infants. And as she approached the ponds, the bones were larger – just as dead, but the bones of older calves and adults.

The tundra here was badly trampled, and all but stripped bare of grass and shrubs; even months of growth hadn't been enough for it to recover. And the bones, too, were badly scattered and trampled. She found crushed skulls, ribs smashed and scored with the marks of mammoth soles. And there were snapped-off tusks, evidence of brief and bitter battles.

There had been little Remembering here, she saw with sadness. It was as the Cycle teaches: *Where water vanishes, sanity soon follows.*

It was becoming horribly clear what had happened here.

As the pressure to find water had grown, so the discipline of this Family had broken down. Probably the youngest – pushed away from the waterholes by their older siblings, even their parents, and too small anyway to reach the water through thick ice with their little tusks – had gone first. Then the oldest and weakest of the adults.

The diminishing survivors had trampled over the bodies of their relatives – perhaps even digging through the fallen corpses to get to the precious liquid – until they, in their turn, had succumbed.

It had been a rich time for the scavengers, and the cubs of Aglu.

The destruction was not thorough; few of the bones close to

the water had been gnawed by the wolves, she saw. But then there had been no need to root in rotting corpses for sustenance; the wolves had only to wait for another mammoth to fall and offer them warm, fresh meat and marrow.

At last she reached the ponds at the grisly heart of this tableau. The ponds brimmed, their surfaces thick with green summer life, swarms of insects buzzing over them. Their fecundity mocked the mammoths who must have come here in the depths of the dry winter, desperate for the water that could have kept them alive.

Silverhair realised that, but for the wisdom of Owlheart, her own Family might have succumbed like this.

Silverhair stood tall, and surveyed the tundra. The land was teeming with life, the hum of insects, the lap of water, the cries of birds and small mammals.

But nowhere was there the voice of a mammoth.

With these bones, Silverhair knew at last that the fears of Lop-ear and Wolfnose were confirmed. Ten thousand years after Longtusk had led his Family here, *there were no more mammoths on the Island*. The winter's dryness had taken the last of the Families – the last but her own.

And now those few survivors were in the hands of the remorseless Lost.

She was alone: the only mammoth in all the world who was alive, and free to act.

She shivered, for she knew that all of her people's history funnelled through her mind and heart now. If she failed, then so would the mammoths, for all time.

. . . And yet, hadn't she already failed? In her foolishness she had ignored the teaching of the Cycle, and had gone to seek out the Lost. And by doing that she had made them aware of the existence of her Family, had caused the deaths of Eggtusk and Lop-ear and Snagtooth and Owlheart, and the trapping of Foxeye and her cubs – all of it was *her fault*.

She sank to the bone-littered ground, heavy with despair.

Alone, desolate, with no Matriarch to guide her – as she'd been trained since she was a calf – she turned to the Cycle.

Mammoths have no gods, no devils. That is why they find it so hard to comprehend the danger posed by the Lost. Instead, mammoths accept their place in the great rhythms of the world, their place in past and future, as Earth's long afternoon winds through the millennia.

But mammoths have existed for a very, very long time; and, the wisdom goes, nothing that happens today is without precedent in the past. Somewhere in the Cycle lies the answer to any question. *Everybody alive is descended from somebody smart enough to survive the past:* that is the underlying message of the Cycle. *But you must not worship your ancestors. The sole purpose of your ancestors' existence was your life. And the sole purpose of your life is your calves'*.

Somehow she felt comforted. Even here, in this place of death, she was not alone; she had the wisdom of all her ancestors back to Kilukpuk, the growing heavy warmth of the creature in her womb, the promise that her calves would one day roam the Sky Steppe.

. . . And that promise, she realised, could only be kept *if Foxeye and the calves were still alive*. For, it seemed, there was no other mammoth Family left anywhere in the world, no other Family which could populate that fabulous land of the future.

In that case, it was up to Silverhair – the last free mammoth – to save her Family from the Lost. She would make her way to the south of the Island, to the foul nest of the Lost. And this time she would enter it, not as a weakened, starved captive, but strong and free. She would destroy Skin-of-Ice and all his works. She would keep her promise to Foxeye and free her Family. And then—

And then, the Cycle would guide her once more into the unknown future.

Treading carefully between the scattered heaps of bones, she resumed her steady march south.

Chapter Five

THE UNDERSEA TUNDRA

At last, after many empty days, she reached the southern coast.

Once more she tramped along the narrow shingle beach. The sky was littered with scattered, glowing clouds, and the calm, flat seascape of floating ice pans perfectly mirrored the sky. Brown kelp streamers lay thickly on the moist stones.

She moved with great caution as she neared the site of the Lost nest, and listened hard for the clattering flap of the light-bird. Her heart pumped. She knew that her best chance would be to surprise the Lost, to charge into their camp and overwhelm them with her flashing tusks.

But there was no noise save the washing of the sea, no smell save the rich salt brine.

No sign of the Lost.

And her plans and speculations dissipated as she reached the nest site.

The camp was abandoned. Only a few blackened scars on the beach showed where the Lost had built their fires; only a few rudimentary shelters remained to show where they had hidden from the rain and wind.

Silverhair ached with frustration. She had been prepared for battle here, and there was no battle to be had. Her blood fizzed through her veins, and her tusks itched with the need to impale the soft belly of a Lost.

She found the stakes to which she had been pinned for so long, still stained black with her blood. And she found the web of black rope which had trapped Foxeye. Rust-brown calf hair was caught in the web. She held the hair to her mouth.

She could taste Sunfire. The Family had been brought here, then.

There was a clatter of whirling wings. She turned, raised her trunk and trumpeted her defiance.

The noise was indeed the light-bird. But it was far away, she saw: on the other side of the Channel, in fact, hovering over the Mainland, which was clear of fog and storm at last; its ugly noise was brought to her by the vagaries of the breezes.

She understood what had happened. The Lost had returned to the Mainland, whence they had come.

There was no sign that the Family had died here; if such a slaughter had taken place the beach would be littered with bones and hair and scraps of flesh and skin. Then – if they were not dead – the mammoths must have been taken to the Mainland too.

If she was to save them, that was where Silverhair must go.

She walked down the beach and stood at the edge of the Channel between Island and Mainland.

In stark contrast to the dry colours of the late-summer landscape, a wide stretch of sea was still white: packed solid by flat ice. Along the shoreline, however, there was a wide band of clear water interspersed with stranded icebergs, many of them grotesquely shaped by continual melting and refreezing. Ivory gulls perched on the highest bergs, and beside the smaller blocks lodged on the tide-line ran little groups of turnstone and sanderling. The wading birds pecked at crustacea among the litter of kelp. The best feeding place for the creatures of the sea was the ice-edge, where the ice met the open sea. She could see many murres working there, their high-pitched calls echoing as their thick bills bobbed into the water. The cries of the birds were overlaid with the deep, powerful breathing of beluga – white whales, their sleek bodies easily as massive as Silverhair's, and capped by a long, spiralling tusk – and narwhal, mottled grey, pods of them cruising the ice-edge or diving beneath the ice itself.

A large bearded seal broke the surface near the coast, regarded Silverhair with big sad eyes, then ducked beneath the ice-strewn water once more.

To get to the Mainland, Silverhair would have to cross this teeming water-world.

She remembered standing on this shore with Lop-ear – her reluctance even to dip her trunk in the sea – his playful calls to the Calves of Siros.

Once, Longtusk had crossed this Channel to bring his Kin to the Island. It had been a great migration, with thousands of mammoths delivered to safety. But the Cycle was silent about how Longtusk did it. Some said he flew across the water. If Silverhair could fly now, she would.

But on one point the Cycle was absolutely clear: Longtusk himself did not survive the passage.

Today, then, she must outdo Longtusk himself.

Silverhair gathered her courage. She stepped forward.

Thin landfast ice crunched around her feet. The water immediately soaked through the thick hair over her legs, and its chill reached her skin. She could feel the water seeping up the hairs dangling from her belly, and more ice broke around her chest.

She stumbled, and suddenly the water flooded over her chest and back and forced its way into her mouth. She scrambled backward, coughing, a spray of water erupting from her mouth. But she lost her footing again and slipped sideways, and suddenly her head was immersed.

She fought brief panic.

She stood straight and lifted her head out of the water, opened her mouth and took a deep draught of air. The water felt tight around her chest, like a band of ice.

Dread flooded her. She remembered the stream of runoff which had almost killed her as a calf. She had been so small then, and the stream – which she could probably ford easily now – had been a lethal torrent, no less intimidating than the Channel which faced her now. She longed to turn and flee back to the land, to abandon this quest.

But she knew this was only the beginning.

Deliberately she took another step forward. The ice, cracking, brushed against her chest. She lifted her head back as far as it could go, trying to keep her eyes and mouth out of the water. But at last the water was too deep, and it closed over her head.

The cold was shocking, like a physical blow, so intense it made her gasp.

She forced herself to open her eyes.

The water was grey-green, and its surface was a glimmering sheet above her. She could see floating ice, thin grey slabs of it over her head.

She thrust her trunk through the surface so that it protruded from the water. She blew, hard, to clear her trunk of water, and sucked in deep lungfuls of clean, salty air. She could feel her chest drag against the heavy pressure of the water, which was trying, it seemed, to crush her ribs like a trampled egg. But she could breathe.

She was floating in the water, submerged save for her trunk, her body hair waving around her. Instinctively she surged forward, dragging at the water with her forelegs, kicking with her hind legs. Soon she could see how she was pushing through the clumps of ice which littered the surface, and the air was whistling easily into her lungs.

Now all she had to do was keep this up for the unknown time it would take to cross the Channel – and overcome the savage current and whatever other dangers might lurk in the deeper water – and emerge, exhausted, on to a beach crawling with Lost . . .

Enough. She clung to the Cycle. *You can only take one breath at a time.* Her other problems could wait until she faced them.

On she swam, into the silent dark, alone.

The sun was low to the west, and it showed as a glimmering disc suspended above the water's rippling surface. She knew that as long as she kept the sun's disc to her right side, she would continue to head south, towards the Mainland.

Away from the coast the pack ice formed a more solid mass, though there were still leads of open water, and holes broken through by melting, or perhaps by seals and bears.

She took a deep breath, pulled down her trunk, and ducked beneath the ice. She would have to swim underwater between the air holes as if she were a seal herself.

She drifted under a ceiling of ice that stretched as far as she could see. There was a carpet of green-brown algae clinging to the ceiling, turning the light a dim green; but in places where the algae grew more thinly, the light came through a clearer blue-white.

And there were creatures grazing on this inverted underwater tundra: tiny shrimp-like creatures which clung to the algae ceiling, and comb jellies which drifted by, trailing long tentacles. She could see how the tentacles were coated with fine, hair-like cilia which pulsed in the current, sparkling with fragmented colour.

The comb jellies, unperturbed by the strange, clumsy intruder, sailed off into the darker water like the shadows of clouds.

She approached an air hole. The sunlit water under the hole was bright with dust. But when she drew near she saw that the 'dust' was a crowd of tiny, translucent animals. She reached the air hole and her head bobbed out of the water's chill, oily calm into the chaotic clamour of light above—

And a polar bear's upraised paw cuffed at her head.

Silverhair trumpeted in alarm.

The bear, just as startled, slithered backwards over the ice floe, its black eyes fixed on this unexpected intruder.

Silverhair panted, her breath frosting. 'Sorry I'm not a fat seal for you,' she said. And she took another deep breath, and ducked back into the sea's oleaginous gloom.

The going got harder as she headed further out to sea.

The ice was very thick here, and huge water-carved blocks and pinnacles were suspended from the ceiling. Salty brine, trapped within the ice, was leaking down to cause this strange, beautiful effect. It was like swimming through a series of caves.

She had to swim an alarmingly long way between air holes.

Once a seal fearlessly approached Silverhair. It seemed to swim with barely a flick of its sleek body – an embarrassing comparison to Silverhair's untidy scrambling – and the ringed pattern of its skin rippled in the water. The seal studied her with jet-black eyes, then turned and swam lazily into the murky distance.

She neared the ice-edge with relief, for she would be able to breathe continually when she passed it. But there was a great deal of activity here. She glimpsed the white shapes of beluga whales sliding in a neat diamond formation through the water. Occasionally there were the brief, spectacular dives of birds hunting fish, explosions from the world of light and air above into this calm darkness.

She drove herself on, past the ice-edge, and into open water.

There was no ice above her now, and no bottom visible beneath her, and she soon left behind the busy life of the ice-edge: there was just herself, alone, suspended in an unending three-dimensional expanse of chill, resisting water.

The current here, far from the friction of the banks of the Channel, was much stronger, and she struggled to keep to her course. And, as she swam on, she could feel the heat of her body leaching out into this unforgiving sea.

As her warmth leaked away, her energy seemed to dissipate with it.

It was as if this infinity of murky, chill water was the only world she had ever known: as if the world above of air and sunlight and snow, of play and love and death, was just some gaudy dream she had enjoyed before waking to this bleak reality . . .

Suddenly her trunk filled with water. She coughed, expelling the water through her mouth. She scrabbled at the water until she was able to raise her face and mouth above the surface. She opened her mouth to take a deep, wheezing breath, and glimpsed a deep-blue sky.

She must have weakened – let herself sink – perhaps even, bizarrely, slept for a heartbeat.

But already she was sinking again.

She continued to kick, but her legs were exhausted. And when she tried to raise her trunk, she couldn't reach the air. The surface was receding from her, slow as a setting sun.

Waterlogged, she was sinking. And hope seeped out of her with the last of her warmth. She would die here, in this endless waste of water, she and her calf.

So the Cycle, after all, culminated in a lie: there would be no rescue for her Family, no glowing future for the mammoths on the Sky Steppe.

She found herself thinking of Lop-ear, that first time they had come to the southern coast: how, in the sunshine, he had teased her and tried to goad her into the water, and told her tall stories of the Calves of Siros. If she had shared Lop-ear's gift for original thinking, was there any way she could have avoided this fate?

. . . *The Calves of Siros*. Suddenly, sinking in the darkness and the cold, she had an idea.

She tried to remember the sounds Lop-ear had made when he had called for the Calves of Siros. She had to get it right; she had only one lungful of air, and would get only one chance at this.

She began a low-pitched whistle, punctuated by higher squeals, squawks and shrieks. The sound rippled away into the black water around her. She kept up the noise until the last wisp of her air was expended.

But not even an echo replied.

She stopped kicking, and let the current carry her. She had fallen so far now the surface was reduced to a vague illumination far above. She could feel the ocean turn her slowly around, as she drifted with it.

A deeper blackness was closing around her vision. The pain in her empty lungs, the ache of her exhausted limbs, the vaguer ache of the wounds inflicted by the Lost – all of it began to recede from her, as the cold forced her to shrink deep into the core of her body.

It was almost comfortable. She knew this ordeal would not last much longer.

. . . And now a sheet of hard blackness rose from the depths beneath her. Perhaps this was death, come to meet her.

But she hadn't expected death to have sleek fur, a fluked tail, stubby flippers, and a small, seal-like head which peered up at her out of the gloom.

The rising surface pushed softly against her feet and belly. She could feel a great body swathed in fat, strong muscles working.

And suddenly she was rising again.

She burst into light and air. It was like being born. She coughed, clearing water from her trunk and mouth, and air roared into her starved lungs.

Gradually, the pain in her chest subsided. She was still floating in the water, but now her trunk lay against a great black body, and she was able to hold herself out of the ocean easily. Strong tail flukes held up her head, and the skin under her face was rough as bark.

The creature under her was huge, she realised: at least twice her own body length, and covered with the dense black hair of a seal.

A small head twisted back to look at her. She heard squeals and chirrups, alternating low whistles and high-toned bleats. It was *speech:* indistinct but nevertheless recognisable.

'. . . See you I. Paddling through water see you I. Recognise mammoth I. Mammoth better swimmer than old sea cow think I. Understand you?'

'Yes,' Silverhair said, and the effort of speech made her cough again. 'I understand. Thanks . . .'

The sea cow's long muscles rippled. To Silverhair's surprise, a gull came flapping out of the sky and landed in the middle of the sea cow's broad back. The gull started to peck at the damp hair there, plucking out parasites, and the sea cow wriggled with pleasure. 'You here are why? Not roll on tundra do sea cows.' And the sea cow raised her small muzzle and whistled at her own joke.

'I have to get to the Mainland,' said Silverhair.

'Mainland? Kelp good there. Mmm. Kelp.' The sea cow looked dreamy. 'But not there go sea cows. Why? *Lost* there.'

'You know about the Lost?'

'Lost? Find me they if, drag me from sea they, eat my kidneys they, leave handsome body for gulls they. Terrible, terrible.'

'I have met the Lost,' said Silverhair.

'Think sea cows all gone Lost. Live in seas in south some Cousins. Here think kill us Lost, long time ago gobble up our kidneys Lost. But wrong they. But not Mainland go to I, kelp or no. Stay by Island. On Island no Lost.'

'There are now,' said Silverhair grimly.

'Terrible, terrible,' said the sea cow, sounding dismayed. 'Go to Mainland you, why if Lost there?'

'I have to,' said Silverhair. 'They took my Family.'

The sea cow rolled in the water, almost throwing Silverhair off. 'Terrible thing. Terrible Lost. Here. Hold on to me you.' And she held out a stubby, clawed flipper. Silverhair wrapped her trunk around it.

The broad flukes beat, sending up a spray which splashed over Silverhair. The sea cow's broad, streamlined bulk began to slide easily through the water, oblivious to the current which had defeated Silverhair, unimpeded even by the bulk of an adult mammoth clinging to one flipper. Soon her speed was so great that a bow wave washed around her small, determined head.

Her power was exhilarating.

*

The sea cow pushed easily through the loose, decaying landfast ice that fringed the shore of the Mainland.

Silverhair's feet crunched on hard shingle.

She let go of the sea cow's flipper. She stumbled forward up a steepening slope, until she had dragged herself clear of the sea. Already frost was forming on her soaked fur, and she shook herself vigorously. Soon the warmth of the afternoon summer sun was seeping into her.

The sea cow used her stubby flippers to haul herself further out of the water, so her bulk was lying on the shingle bed, her great broad back exposed. She began munching contentedly on a floating scum of brown kelp fronds. She chewed with a horny plate at the front of her mouth, for she didn't appear to have any teeth. 'Kelp. Mmm. Want some you?'

'Thanks – no.'

Now she was raised so far out of the water, Silverhair could see how strange the sea cow looked: a head and flippers much like a seal's, but trailing a great bulbous body and a powerful split fluke, as if the front half of a seal had been attached to a beluga whale. Out of the water she was ponderous and looked stranded. Silverhair could see why her kind had been such easy pickings for the Lost, before the sea cows had learned to hide and feign extinction.

Silverhair looked back at the dark, sinuous waters of the Channel. 'But for you,' she told the sea cow, 'I'd still be out there now. There for ever.'

The sea cow's fluke beat at the water. 'Oath of Kilukpuk. Hyros and Probos and Siros. Forgot that you?'

'No,' said Silverhair quietly. 'No, we haven't forgotten.' And she was filled with warmth as she realised that one of the most ancient and beautiful passages of the Cycle had been fulfilled, here on this desolate beach.

The Calves of Kilukpuk had been separated for more than fifty million years. But they hadn't forgotten their Oath.

The sea cow rolled gracefully and slid into deeper water. 'Stick to tundra next time you. Watch out for Lost you. Good luck, Cousin.' Her stubby flippers extended, and she slid beneath the ice-strewn waves.

And Silverhair, her trunk raised and every half-frozen hair prickling, walked slowly up the shingle beach, into the land of the Lost.

Chapter Six

THE CITY OF THE LOST

Everywhere on this ugly Mainland beach there was evidence of the Lost: chunks of rusting metal, splashes of dirty oil which stained the ice, scraps of the strange loose outer skin they wore. There were structures, long and narrow, which pushed out from the beach towards the water; at the end of these structures were more of the shell-like objects like the one she had seen on the ice floe, on her first encounter with Skin-of-Ice. But where the thing on that ice floe had been damaged, these seemed intact; they floated on the grey water, though some were embedded in the ice. Perhaps they were supposed to ferry the Lost across the water, she mused.

She walked over a line of scrubby dunes at the edge of the beach, and reached the tundra. There was grass and sedge, and even a few Arctic willows; but the ground was poor – polluted by more of the black sludgy oil which had marred the beach – and broken up by long, snaking tracks. There was a stink of tar, and a strange silence, an emptiness that was a chilling contrast to the Island's rich summer cacophony.

And everywhere there were straight lines: the hard signature of the Lost, the symbol of their dominance over the world around them.

The most gigantic line of all was a hard-edged surface set in the tundra, black and lifeless. It was a road that proceeded – straight as a shaft of sunlight – to the heart of the City of the Lost.

The City itself was the sight she had seen many times from the safety of the headland on the Island: a tangle of shining tubes and tanks, randomly cross-connected, sprinkled with glowing point lights, like captive stars. From tall columns oily black smoke billowed into the air, its tarry stink overpowering even the sharp tang of brine.

The City was huge, sprawling over the tundra. It must be the Lost's prime nest, she thought. And that was where she must go.

She stepped away from the road. She found a place where the tundra wasn't quite so badly scarred, and there was grass and willow twigs to graze. She deliberately pushed the food into her mouth, ground it up and swallowed it. She found a stream. It was thin and brackish, but it tasted clean; the cold water seemed to revive her strength a little.

She noticed a carpet of lemming holes and runs, and droppings from the predator birds which hunted the little rodents. So there was life here.

And she glimpsed an Arctic fox, the last of its white winter fur clinging to its back. The fox's coat was patchy and discoloured, the nodes of its spine protruding from its back. As soon as the fox saw her, its hairs stood on end. Then it dropped its muzzle, as if in shame, and slunk away.

Silverhair thought she understood. This creature had abandoned the tundra and had learned to live in the corners of the world of the Lost. But it was a poor bargain. She wondered if, in some deep recess of its hind brain, the fox still longed for the open freedom and rich, clean silence of the tundra its ancestors had abandoned.

Her feeding done, she passed dung, the movement fast and satisfying. The world seemed vivid around her, ugly and distorted as it was here on the Mainland. If this was to be her day to die then there would be a last time for everything: to love, to eat, even to pass dung – and at last to breathe. And all of it should be cherished, for death was long.

The rich scent of her own dung filled her nostrils – and suddenly she realised that *there was no smell of mammoth here.*

The mammoths had seeped into every crevice of their Island. It wasn't possible to pull up a blade of grass which hadn't been nourished by the dung of mammoths; mammoth bones erupted from the ground everywhere as the permafrost melted; mammoths had even shaped the tundra itself, by battering down the encroaching trees of the spruce forest.

But that wasn't true here. When she raised her trunk to the air and sniffed, all she could smell was smoke and tar. And this was the place to which Foxeye and her calves had been brought: the place from which Silverhair must rescue them, or die in the attempt.

Perhaps if Lop-ear was here, she thought wistfully, he might be able to devise some plan, some way to gain an advantage over these unknowable swarms of Lost. But he wasn't here, and she had no plan. She could only rely on her strength and speed and courage and native intelligence – and the guidance of the Cycle, which had brought her this far.

She walked back to the Lost road. Its hard surface was unyielding under the pads of her feet, and its blackness soaked up the thin rays of the sun, making it feel hot. She recoiled from its strangeness.

But she raised her trunk, every sense alert, and began to walk.

The City of the Lost sprawled across the landscape, ugly, careless, uncompromising. It was a place of huge rust-stained cylinders, gigantic pipes that littered the ground, smaller tanks and boxes and heaps of strange metal shapes. As she approached the City's heart, the tallest buildings loomed over her, and she felt a helpless awe at their tall, shadowy straightness – and at the power of the worm-like creatures who had built this place.

But it was a place of waste.

She came to a pile of spruce wood, cut, evidently with great effort, into lengths – and then abandoned on the ground to rot. And here was a heap of cracked-open cans that had been evidently simply abandoned, piled up without purpose or value. Traces of brown, rotting metal and oil had leaked into the ground, poisoning it so nothing grew here.

The Lost were *not* like the mammoths, she thought, whose very dung enriched the places they passed.

. . . And now, suddenly, she encountered her first Lost.

He came walking around one of the buildings, not looking up, his face lowered so he could peer at a sheet he carried. His outer skin was a gaudy blue, and he wore some form of orange carapace, hard and shiny, on his head.

She stood stock still, her trunk and tusks raised high above him.

His footsteps slowed, halted. Perhaps it was her smell he had noticed – or even the stink of brine which she must have carried from the sea.

He turned, slowly. He lowered his sheet, revealing cold blue eyes.

Silverhair saw herself through his eyes. Perhaps she was the first mammoth he had ever seen. She loomed before him like a fur-covered mountain, stinking of brine, her tusks alone almost as long as his body. And her face was a scarred mask, from which hard, determined eyes glowered.

The Lost yelped, comically. He threw his sheet up in the air, and stumbled backwards, landing in the mud.

He scrambled to his feet and ran away along the road, yelling. He turned a corner and disappeared into the complex, shadowy heart of the City. The sheet he had discarded blew towards her feet; she crushed it with one deliberate footstep.

Stolidly, she followed the fleeing Lost.

The buildings of the Lost loomed huge and faceless, dwarfing her. The only sounds were her own breathing, the soft slap of her footsteps – and the thumping of some distant metal heart, its low growl deeper than the deepest contact rumble. This place was *alive*, and she was willingly walking into its mouth.

And suddenly the Lost were here. Evidently Orange-Head had raised a warning. She was faced by a row of them – three, four, five, emerging from the buildings – and they all looked scared, even though they bore thunder-sticks aimed at her chest and head.

She had known this confrontation would come. She was a mammoth: not a burrowing lemming, a scurrying fox who could hide.

And she knew that from this point, the river of time, running to eternity, would split into two branches.

If the Lost chose to pump her body full of the stinging pellets of their thunder-sticks, then she would die here – though she would, she thought grimly, take as many of them with her as possible. But if not . . .

If not, if she lived and the future was still open, there was hope.

She took a deliberate step forward, towards the circle of Lost.

One thunder-stick cracked. A pellet sizzled past her ear. She couldn't help but flinch.

But it had missed her. Still she stepped forward.

Now the Lost were cawing to each other. One of them seemed to be taking command, and was waving his paws at the others. One by one, uncertainly, they lowered their thunder-sticks. Evidently they didn't want to kill her. Not yet, anyway.

Perhaps they had their own purpose for her. Well, she didn't care about that. For now, it was enough that she still breathed.

She called with the contact rumble: 'Foxeye! Croptail! Can you hear me? It's Silverhair. Foxeye, call if you hear me . . .'

She heard the thin trumpeting of a frightened calf – a trumpeting that was cut off abruptly.

Her heart hammered. At least one of them was still alive, then.

She moved forward, gliding deeper into the complex of buildings and pipes and smoking pillars. The Lost formed up behind her, their thunder-sticks never far below their shoulders, and they followed her like a gaggle of ugly calves. She called as she walked, and liquid mammoth rumbles echoed from the metal walls of this City of the Lost, and the massive, natural grace of her gait contrasted with the angular ugliness of the place.

She walked right through the City, to its far side.

Here she could see open tundra, stretching away. There were more buildings here, but their character was different. These were much rougher structures, some of them so flimsy they looked ready to fall down. Thin smoke snaked up to the grey sky, bearing the sour smell of burned meat. The ground here was churned-up, lifeless mud.

There were many Lost here, some of them emerging from the crude buildings to stare at her, some running away in fear.

And there, in a clearing at the centre of this cluster of buildings, were the mammoths. She counted quickly – Foxeye and Croptail and Sunfire – all of them alive, if miserable and bedraggled. Her heart hammered, and she longed to rush forward to her Family. But she forced herself to be still, to observe, to think.

The mammoths were held in two cages: one for Foxeye alone, the other for the two calves. When the calves saw Silverhair approach, Croptail set up an excited squealing. 'Silverhair!'

The cages, crudely constructed, were too small to allow the mammoths to move, even to turn around. They had thick ropes trailing from their roofs. Silverhair saw how distressed the calves were to be separated from their mother. Silverhair wondered if these Lost knew how cruel that separation was – indeed, that without her mother's milk Sunfire would soon surely die.

Croptail was still calling. But there was a Lost beside the calves' cage. He had a goad which he flicked cruelly through the bars of the cage, snapping at Croptail's flank.

Silverhair rumbled threateningly.

The Lost looked at her – an unrestrained adult mammoth – and decided not to whip the trapped calf again.

Silverhair approached Foxeye's cage. Foxeye was standing with her great head bowed, beaten and subdued, her coat filthy. She was burdened by heavy chains which looped around her neck and feet, fixed to stakes rammed into the muddy ground. Silverhair reached through the bars of the cage, and wrapped her trunk around Foxeye's.

At first Foxeye's trunk was limp. But then, slowly, it tightened.

'I promised I'd save you,' said Silverhair. 'And here I am.'

'We thought you were dead,' Foxeye said, almost inaudibly.

'You were almost right,' said Silverhair dryly. 'But we're still alive.'

'For now,' said Foxeye dully.

Deliberately, slowly, still trying not to alarm the Lost with their thunder-sticks, Silverhair turned and wrapped her trunk around the stakes which bound her sister's chains. The stakes were fixed only loosely in the ground, and were easy to tug free of the mud.

'Help me, Foxeye.'

'I can't . . .'

'You can. For the calves. Come on . . .'

With their sensitive trunk-fingers, the sisters explored the cage. Silverhair found twists of thick wire; the wire was easy to manipulate, and when it was gone, the front of the cage fell away into the mud.

At first Foxeye cowered in the back of her open cage. But then she allowed herself to be led, by Silverhair's gentle tugs at her trunk, out of the cage.

The Lost seemed surprised by the ability of the mammoths to take the cage apart, and they were arguing, perhaps trying to decide whether to use their thunder-sticks.

Silverhair tugged Foxeye to the calves' cage. The heavy chains at Foxeye's neck and legs clanked, trailing in the mud, and as they approached, the Lost who had goaded Croptail ran off.

The calves were not chained up, and Silverhair and Foxeye simply lifted the cage up and off them. Croptail and Sunfire rushed to their mother; Sunfire immediately found a teat to suckle.

Silverhair made sure she threw the cage impressively far before letting it crash to the mud. It collapsed with a clatter of metal, sending more of the Lost fleeing.

She nudged Foxeye. 'Come on. We can't wait here.'

Croptail poked his head out from under his mother's belly hair. 'What's the plan, Silverhair?'

No plan, she thought. *I'm no Lop-ear* . . . 'We're just going to walk right out of here. Don't be afraid.'

She turned and faced the Lost. She looked around at their empty faces, their skinny bodies, their dangling jaws. She had the impression that these were not truly evil creatures – at least, not all of them. Just – Lost.

'Listen to me,' she said. 'Perhaps you can understand some of what I say. I am not going to permit you to take my Family away from their home. And if you try to stop us, I promise you your families will have to perform many Rememberings.'

But the Lost merely stared at her trumpeting, foot-stamping and rumbling, as if it wasn't a language at all.

She turned back to her Family. 'Go,' she said. 'You first, Croptail. That way – out to the tundra. We won't go through the City again. We'll make for the shore.'

'Then what?' demanded Croptail.

'Just do as I say.'

Bemused, frightened, Croptail obeyed. Soon, the little group of mammoths was gliding slowly towards the empty tundra.

As they walked steadily, Silverhair stared at the decrepit buildings, the rows of silent, staring Lost. 'This is a hellish place,' she said.

'Yes,' said Foxeye. 'I've been watching them. I think they want to turn the whole Earth into a gigantic city like this. Soon there will be nothing living but the Lost and the rodents that scurry for their scraps . . .'

She told Silverhair how the mammoths had been brought here.

After their capture in the ice chasm, they had been taken

back to the beach and bound up tightly, with ropes and chains. Then harnesses had been fixed around them, and they had been attached to the light-bird with its whirling wings – and, one by one, lifted into the sky.

'Mammoths aren't meant to fly, sister,' said Foxeye, and Silverhair could hear the dread in her voice. 'The Lost were taken away too. I think the ones who attacked us – Skin-of-Ice and the others – had been somehow stranded on the Island. The light-birds came for them when the storms cleared from the Mainland.'

'What do the Lost intend now?'

'They don't seem to want to kill us. Not right away. They have plenty to eat here, Silverhair; they don't need our flesh, nor our bones to burn . . .'

'There was rope fixed to your cage.'

'Yes. I think they were going to move us again. Fly us. Perhaps take us far from the tundra. Somewhere where there are many, many Lost, more Lost than all the mammoths who ever lived. And they would come and see us in our cages, and hit us with sticks, for they were never, ever going to let us out of there again.'

'Foxeye—'

'I'd have given up my calves,' Foxeye blurted. 'If I could have spoken to the Lost, if I thought they would have spared me, I'd have given up the calves. There: what do you think of me now?'

Silverhair rubbed her sister's filth-matted scalp. 'I think I got here just in time.'

The little group walked steadily onward, through the clutter of buildings, towards the tundra. Silverhair was dimly aware of more light-birds clattering over her head. She flinched, expecting an attack from that quarter. But none came. The birds seemed to be descending towards the City, and some of the Lost who had followed the mammoths were pointing up with their paws, muttering. Perhaps this was some new group of Lost, she thought; perhaps the Lost were divided amongst themselves.

It scarcely mattered. What was important was that still none of them tried to stop her.

Silverhair took one step after another, aware how little control she had over events, scarcely daring to hope she could take another breath. But they were still alive, and free. By Kilukpuk's hairy navel, she thought, this might actually work.

But then there was a roar like an angry god, and everything fell apart.

A Lost came running forward, face red with rage. In one paw he held a glinting flask of the clear inflaming liquid. And he carried a thunder-stick which he fired wildly.

This was a new type of stick, Silverhair realised immediately: one which spoke not with a single shout, but with a roar, and lethal insects poured out in a great cloud. Even the other Lost were forced to scatter as those deadly pellets smacked into the mud, or turned the walls of the crude dwellings into splinters.

The newcomer seemed to be berating the others. And he was turning the spitting nozzle of his thunder-stick towards the huddled Family.

This Lost wasn't going to let the mammoths go; he would obviously rather destroy them.

He was Skin-of-Ice.

Silverhair didn't even think about it. She just lowered her head and charged.

Everything slowed down, as if she were swimming through thick, ice-cold water.

She lowered her tusks, and he raised his thunder-stick, and she looked into his eyes. It was as if they were joined by that gaze, as if total communication were passing between their souls, as if there were nobody else in the universe but the two of them.

She felt a stab of regret to have come so close to freedom. But in her heart she had known it would come to this moment, that she would not survive the day.

If Skin-of-Ice had held his ground and used his thunder-stick he would surely have killed her there and then. But he didn't. In the last heartbeat, as a mountain of enraged mammoth bore down on him, he panicked.

Even as he made his thunder-stick roar, he fell backwards and rolled sideways.

Pain erupted in a line drawn across her face, chest and leg, and she felt her blood spurt, warm. One of the projectiles passed clean through her mouth, in one cheek and out through the other, splintering a tooth.

The pain was extraordinary.

She could hear the screams of Lost and mammoths alike, smell the metallic stink of her own blood. But she was still alive, still moving.

Skin-of-Ice was on the ground, scrabbling for his thunder-stick. She stood over him.

Again, in the face of her courage and strength, he made the wrong decision. If he had abandoned the thunder-stick he might have escaped. But he did not. He had waited too long.

Silverhair lowered her tusk and speared him cleanly through the upper hind leg.

He screamed, and reached behind him to grab her tusk with his paws. She lifted her head, and Skin-of-Ice dangled on her tusk like a shred of winter hair, and she felt a fierce exultation.

But in one paw he held the thunder-stick. It sprayed its

deadly fire in the air. And he kicked; his foot smashed into her forehead, and, with remarkable strength, he dragged his injured leg free of her tusk.

He fell more than twice his height to the ground.

But then he was moving again, firing his thunder-stick. The watching Lost fled, yelling.

Silverhair charged again.

Skin-of-Ice brought the thunder-stick round to point at Silverhair. But he wasn't quick enough.

As she reared over him, a hail of stings poured into her foreleg. She could feel bone shatter, muscles rip to shreds; when she tried to put her weight on that leg she stumbled.

But she had him.

She wrapped her strong trunk around his waist and, trumpeting her rage, hurled him into the air. Skin-of-Ice sailed high, twisting, writhing and firing his thunder-stick. He fell heavily, and she heard a cracking sound.

But still he pushed himself up with his forelegs. She felt a flicker of admiration for his determination. But she knew it was the stubbornness of madness.

She grabbed his hind foot with her trunk. She twisted, and heard bone crunch, ligaments snap. Skin-of-Ice screamed.

She flipped him on to his back, like a seal landing a fish on an ice floe. He still had his thunder-stick, and he raised it at her. But the stick no longer spat its venom. She could see how it was twisted and broken.

Skin-of-Ice hurled the useless stick away, his small face distended with purple rage. Her strength and endurance had, in the end, defeated even its ugly threat.

He tried to rise, but she pushed him back with her trunk. Still he fought, clawing at her trunk as if trying to rip his way through her skin with his bare paws. She leaned forward and rested her tusk against his throat.

For a heartbeat, as Skin-of-Ice fought and spat, she held him. She thought of those who had died at his hands: Owlheart, Eggtusk, Snagtooth, Lop-ear. And she remembered her own hot dreams of destroying this monster.

A single thrust and it would be over.

She released him.

'You Lost are the dealers of death,' she said heavily. 'Not the mammoths.'

Still Skin-of-Ice tried to rise up to attack her. But other Lost came forward and dragged him back.

There were Lost all around Silverhair now, and they were raising their thunder-sticks.

She struggled to rise, to use her one good foreleg to lever herself upright. She could feel the wounds in her chest and leg tear wider, and the pain was sharp. But she would die on her feet.

She wished she could reach her Family, entwine trunks with them one last time.

She wondered why the Lost hadn't destroyed her already. She looked down at them. She saw they were hesitating; some of them had lowered their thunder-sticks.

'. . . Silverhair. Stay still. They won't harm you now. It isn't your day to die, Silverhair . . .'

It was – impossibly – the voice of an adult Bull.

She turned. A Lost was coming towards her: a new kind, all in white. He held his cupped paws up to his mouth, and he was shouting at the other Lost, making them turn their thunder-sticks away.

'. . . Don't be afraid. The Family will be safe. Nobody else will die today . . .'

And with the Lost there was a mammoth, without chains or ropes or any restraints, a mammoth who walked unhindered through the circle of thunder-sticks with this strange, posturing Lost.

It was a Bull, with one limp and damaged ear.

It was Lop-ear.

Chapter Seven

THE CALVES OF PROBOS

Silverhair walked forward, over the soft, marshy ground of the Island.

Autumn was coming. The sun had lost its warmth, and was once more sliding beneath the horizon each night. There was no true darkness yet, but there would be long hours of spectral, indigo twilight before the sun returned. The birches, willows and other plants had started to turn to their autumn colours: crimson, ochre, yellow, vermilion, russet brown and even gold. The air was peaceful, musty with the smell of leaves and fungus. But the nights had turned cold, the frost riming the ground. And the ponds had started to freeze again, from their edges; each night's increment was marked by lines in the ice, like the growth rings of a tusk.

The land was emptying. The first migrating birds were already starting to abandon the tundra for their winter homes to the south: great flocks of swans, geese and sandpipers. Soon the silence of winter would return to the Island, and the summer's colour and noise would be as remote as a dream.

But this was like no other autumn. For Silverhair knew that the plain was barred from her by the walls the Lost had built around them: *glass*, Lop-ear had called this strange, hard, clear stuff. And in the distance she could see teams of the Lost moving about the Island's tundra, on foot or in their strange clattering vehicles.

Silverhair found a rich tuft of grass. She bent to pluck it up with her trunk, but as she tried to bend her knee her damaged leg rippled with pain. The white stuff the strange Lost had wrapped around her leg – while Lop-ear had been steadily persuading her not to gore him – was still in place, but it was threadbare and dirty, and she could see blood seeping through it.

Still, her leg was healing. There was no denying the Lost were clever. Not wise – but clever.

She heard a miniature trumpeting, a small rumble of protest. She glanced around. The calves were wrestling again; Sunfire, growing quickly, was almost as large as her brother now, and it was all Foxeye could do to separate them.

After her final battle with the Lost called Skin-of-Ice, the mammoths had been taken back to the Island across the Channel, in one of the peculiar floating metal bergs. Then – under the gentle supervision of the Lost – they had walked north, to this glassy enclosure.

The Family had never been so well fed, so safe from the attentions of predators. But Silverhair knew she would never be comfortable again, for she was living at the sufferance of the Lost.

Even if they had given Lop-ear back to her.

'. . . Not all the Lost are evil, Silverhair,' Lop-ear was saying. 'You must remember that. I've been observing them, trying to understand. Just as mammoths differ in personality, so do the Lost.'

'Lop-ear,' she said reasonably, 'they tried to kill you.'

'The actions of a few Lost don't reflect on the whole species. The Lost we encountered – Skin-of-Ice and his cronies – shouldn't even have been here on the Island. They are criminals. They were smuggling the clear liquid we saw them drink—'

'The stuff that makes them crazy.'

'They were blown to the Island in a storm. They were stranded here for most of the summer by the storms on the Mainland. They were starving; they can't graze grass or hunt as the wolves can. They even tried to eat the meat of the ancient mammoths that emerge from the permafrost, but it made them ill. And so when they found us—'

'The Cycle teaches us that the belly of a wolf is a noble grave,' Silverhair growled. 'Maybe that's true of the shrivelled belly of a Lost too. It doesn't mean I have to welcome it.

'And besides, it wasn't their butchery that bothered me. Lop-ear, the Lost tried to kill you for no reason other than a lust for blood. They would have tortured me until I submitted to them like poor Snagtooth, or until I died. How can we share a world with creatures like that?'

'Because we must,' said Lop-ear bluntly. 'For the world is theirs. You have to understand there are lots of . . . *groups* among these Lost. And they pursue different goals.

'First there was Skin-of-Ice and his gang of criminals, with their angry-making water, and their need to survive. When the weather broke the criminals were rescued by another group, the workers from the City of the Lost. And the workers saw an opportunity in us. They didn't want to kill us or eat us, but they did think they could give us to others of their kind.'

'*Give* us to them? What for? Why?'

'So we could be – displayed,' he said. 'To great groups of Lost, young and old—'

Just as Foxeye had suspected. 'So,' Silverhair said bitterly, 'the Lost can mock the creatures from whom they stole the planet.'

'Something like that, I suppose. But there was *another* group of Lost, who had been here on the Island long before all the others. They built the Nest of Straight Lines. They kept others away from the Island for years, and they didn't have any curiosity about what lay in the Island's interior. They just stayed put and did their work.'

'What work?'

'How can I know that? You see, after the time of Longtusk, the Lost thought there were no more mammoths left anywhere in the world. They thought the Island was empty, and that's why, for half a Great-Year, they didn't even come looking for us.

'And then there's *another* group – I know it's confusing, Silverhair – the ones who have saved us. And those Lost *care* about us.

'Somehow they heard that we had been discovered by the criminals. They came here, found me and saved my life – I tell you, Silverhair, after I got away from Skin-of-Ice I was ready for Remembering, I was eating my hair and speaking gibberish to the lemmings – and then they came to the Mainland to search for the rest of the Family.'

'They were nearly too late,' said Silverhair grimly.

'That's true,' he said. 'With more time the workers from the City of the Lost would have flown the others away – or else killed them. If not for you. You saved them, Silverhair. You saved the future.'

'Only to deliver us into the paws of more Lost.'

He eyed her. 'You still blame yourself, don't you?'

'If I hadn't gone seeking out the Lost in that blundering way – if I'd listened to Eggtusk and Owlheart – they might still be alive now.'

'No,' he said firmly. 'The Lost would have found us anyway. They'd already discovered the body in the *yedoma*, remember. We could no more have evaded them than we could a swarm of mosquitoes, and the mammoths would have been destroyed anyway. What you did gave us enough warning to act, to save ourselves. And besides, these new Lost—'

'These new Lost are *different*,' she said with heavy sarcasm.

'So they are,' he said, exasperated. 'Watch this.' And he trotted forward to the glass wall surrounding them, and touched it with his trunk.

The wall shimmered, and filled with light.

Silverhair gasped and stumbled backwards.

There was light all around her. A fat sun – brilliant, brighter than any Arctic sun – beat down from a washed-out brown-white sky. The ground was a baked plain, where black-leafed trees and stunted bushes struggled to grow. The horizon was muddied by a rippling shimmer of heated air. There was a smell of burning, far off on the breeze.

This was a huge, old land, she suspected.

Lop-ear was at her side. 'Don't be alarmed. It isn't real. We're still on the Island, in the glass box on the tundra. And yet—'

'What?'

'And yet it *is* real. In a way. The Lost have made this thing, this strange powerful wall, so we could see this place, even smell its dust . . .'

'What place?'

'Silverhair, this is a land far away – far to the south, where ice never comes and it never grows cold.'

A contact rumble came washing over the empty ground.

'*Mammoths*,' she hissed.

'Not exactly.'

And now she saw them: dark shapes moving easily on the horizon, like drifting boulders, huge ears flapping.

One of them turned, as if to face her. It was a Cow. She seemed to be hairless, and her bare skin was like weatherbeaten wood. She had no tusks. There was a calf at her side.

Behind her, a Family was walking. No, more than a Family – a *Clan*, perhaps, for there were hundreds of them, the young clustering around the Matriarchs, Bulls flanking the main group. Silverhair could hear liquid contact rumbles, trumpets and high-pitched squeaks; the Earth seemed to shake with the passage of those giant feet.

'They can't see us,' Lop-ear said softly.

'They are beautiful. Perhaps Meridi looked like this.'

'Yes. Perhaps.'

'Are they real?'

'Oh, yes,' said Lop-ear. 'They are real. Real – but not free, despite the way it looks. Silverhair, these are *elephants*.'

'Calves of Probos.'

'Yes. Just as we are. They are many, we are few. But, despite their greater numbers, these Cousins too are under threat from the expansion of the Lost. But the Lost have protected them, and studied them.

'Look – one Family isn't enough to continue the mammoths. Despite all we've achieved, we would die here on the Island, after another generation, two.'

'I know. We need fresh blood.'

'And it is our new Cousins who will provide it. I have seen what the Lost are trying to do, and I think I understand. These Cousins are sufficiently like us for the Lost to be able to mix our blood with theirs . . .'

'*Mix our blood?*'

'Something like that. The Lost are trying to assure our future, Silverhair.'

The big Cow turned away from them. She reached down to wrap an affectionate trunk around her suckling calf, and walked on, the calf scurrying at her feet.

Lop-ear touched the wall again and the strange scene disappeared, revealing the windswept tundra once more.

None of the elephants had tusks, Silverhair noted sadly. They had survived, but they had been forced to make their bargain with the Lost.

'Perhaps these Lost really do mean us well,' she said. 'But—'

'Yes?'

'But they will never let us go. Will they?'

'They *can't*, Silverhair. Earth is crowded with Lost. There is no room for us.'

At sunset, the weather broke.

Rain began to beat down, and Silverhair knew it was likely to continue for days. A grey mist hung over the green meadows, and the moisture gave the air a texture of mystery and tragedy. It was beautiful, but Silverhair knew what it meant. 'The end of another summer,' she said. 'It goes so quickly. And winter is so long . . .'

Silverhair knew her story was nearly over.

Skin-of-Ice had done her a great deal of damage – she could feel the deep unclosed wounds inside her – damage that couldn't be put right, regardless of the clever ministrations of these new Lost. There was only one more summer left in her, perhaps two. But she had no complaint; that would be enough for her to bear and suckle her calf, and teach it the stories from the Cycle.

She even knew what she would call the calf, such was its great weight in her belly. *Icebones*.

She knew she could never forgive the Lost for the things they had done to her and her Family. Perhaps it was just as well she would soon take that antiquated hatred to her grave.

For the future belonged to the calves, as it always had.

Lop-ear seemed to know what she was thinking . He stood beside her and rubbed her back with his trunk. 'We really are the last, you know. The last of the mammoths.'

'All those who had to die – Eggtusk, Owlheart, Snag-tooth—'

'They did not die in vain,' he said gently. 'Every one of them died bravely, fighting to preserve the Family. We will always Remember them.

'But now we have the future ahead of us. And you're the Matriarch, Silverhair. Just as Owlheart predicted.' He rubbed her belly, over the bump of the unborn calf there. 'It's up to you to keep the Cycle alive, and help us remember the old ways. Then we'll be ready when our time comes again.'

'I don't think I have the strength any more, Lop-ear.'

'You do. You know you do. And you'll be remembered. The Cycle – our history – stretches back in time across twenty thousand great years. Its songs tell of the exploits of many heroes. But in all that immense chronicle, there is no hero to match you, Silverhair. One day our calves will run freely on the Sky Steppe, and their lives will be rich beyond our imagining. But they will envy you. For you were the most important mammoth of all. Cupped in the palm of history, caught between past and future, your actions shaped a world . . .'

She snuggled against him affectionately. 'You always did talk too much, dear Lop-ear. Hush, now.'

The rain lessened, and the scudding clouds broke up, briefly.

The setting sun, swollen in the damp air, cast a pink-red glow which seemed to fill the sky, and the first stars gleamed.

'Look,' said Lop-ear softly, and he tugged her ear.

She looked up. The Sky Steppe was floating high above the moist tundra, a point of light gleaming fiery red. She stared through the glass wall at the ruddy air. It seemed to her that – just for a heartbeat – the red fire of the Sky Steppe washed down over the world, mixing with the sunset.

But then the clouds closed over the sky, and she was looking out at the dullness of the moist, rainy tundra.

Lop-ear was still talking. '. . . strange name, but the Lost—'

'What did you say?'

'I was telling you what the Lost call the Sky Steppe. For they see it better than we do, Silverhair. They know much about the land there, even about the two moons that follow it. They call it—' And he raised his head to the light in the sky, and shaped his mouth to utter the strange Lost sound.

'*Mars.*'

The sky closed over, and snow began to fall steadily. The Arctic summer was over, and Silverhair could feel the bony touch of another long, hard winter.

EPILOGUE

It is a frozen world.

Though the sun is rising, the sky above is still speckled with stars. There is a flat, sharp, close horizon, a plain of dust and rocks. The rocks are carved by the wind. Everything is stained rust brown, like dried blood, the shadows long and sharp.

And in the east there is a morning star: steady, brilliant, its delicate blue-white distinct against the violet wash of the dawn. Sharp-eyed creatures might see that this is a double star: a faint silver-grey companion circles close to its blue master.

The sun continues to strengthen. It is an elliptical patch of yellow light, suspended in a brown sky. But the sun looks small, feeble; this seems a cold, remote place. As the dawn progresses the dust suspended in the air scatters the light and suffuses everything with a pale, salmon hue. At last the gathering light masks the moons.

Two of them.

The land isn't completely flat. There are low sand dunes, and a soft shadow in the sand. It looks like a shallow ridge.

It is the wall of a crater.

It seems impossible that anything should live here. And yet there is life.

Lichen clings to the crater walls, steadily manufacturing oxygen, and there are tufts of hardy grasses. There are even dwarf willow trees, their branches hugging the ground.

. . . And there is more.

A vicious wind is rising, and lifting the dust into a storm. The horizon is lost now in a pink haze, and the world becomes a washed-out bowl of pink light.

And out of that haze something looms: a mountainous shape, seemingly too massive to move, and yet move it does. As it approaches through the obscuring mist, more of its form becomes visible: a body round as an eroded rock, head dropped down before it, the whole covered in a layer of thick red-brown hair.

The great head rears up. A trunk comes questing, and immense tusks sweep. An eye opens, warm, brown, intense, startlingly human.

The great trunk lifts, and the woolly mammoth trumpets her ancient songs of blood and wisdom.

Her name is Icebones.

AFTERWORD

My research for this book took me to the Hwange National Park, Zimbabwe; the Chobe National Park, Botswana; the George C. Page Museum at the Rancho La Brea tar pits, Los Angeles County; the Natural History Museum, London; and the National Museum of Natural History, Washington DC. I'm indebted to Eric Brown for reading the manuscript, and for feedback to Dr Adrian Lister of the Department of Biology, University College, London. Dr Lister's masterly book *Mammoths* (Macmillan, 1994) was an essential resource, as was Gary Haynes's *Mammoths, Mastodons and Elephants* (Cambridge University Press, 1991). Any errors, omissions or misinterpretations are of course mine.

Stephen Baxter
Great Missenden
August 1998